Parrots

Julien L. Bronson

This book originally appeared as *Parrot Family Birds: Their Training, Care and Breeding*. It has been updated and enhanced with beautiful color photographs for this new T.F.H. edition.

Cover photographs: Amazon parrots by Stefan Norberg and Anders Hansson (front) and courtesy of Vogelpark Walsrode (back).

Distributed in the UNITED STATES by T.F.H. Publications, Inc., 211 West Sylvania Avenue, Neptune City, NJ 07753; in CANADA by H & L Pet Supplies Inc., 27 Kingston Crescent, Kitchener, Ontario N2B 2T6; Rolf C. Hagen Ltd., 3225 Sartelon Street, Montreal 382 Quebec; in ENGLAND by T.F.H. Publications Limited, 4 Kier Park, Ascot, Berkshire SL5 7DS; in AUSTRALIA AND THE SOUTH PACIFIC by T.F.H. (Australia) Pty. Ltd., Box 149, Brookvale 2100 N.S.W., Australia; in NEW ZEALAND by Ross Haines & Son, Ltd., 18 Monmouth Street, Grey Lynn, Auckland 2 New Zealand; in SINGAPORE AND MALAYSIA by MPH Distributors (S) Pte., Ltd., 601 Sims Drive, # 03/07/21, Singapore 1438; in the PHILIPPINES by Bio-Research, 5 Lippay Street, San Lorenzo Village, Makati Rizal; in SOUTH AFRICA by Multipet Pty. Ltd., 30 Turners Avenue, Durban 4001. Published by T.F.H. Publications Inc., Ltd. the British Crown Colony of Hong Kong.

Contents

Three species of Australian parrots: the Budgerigar, the Cockatiel, and the Galah.

Tame Parrots

Parrots, or psittacine birds, have been kept as pets for centuries, since the days of ancient Greece and Rome and other civilizations before them. The Grey Parrot was the best known in Europe during those times, and was brought in by the merchant galleys. In India and China, which had older civilizations, the Alexandrine and other asiatic parakeets were kept by the inhabitants. In South America, the Incas and other Indian cultures kept macaws and the various species of amazon parrots.

The most recent and most beautifully colored psittacine birds to become known to man are the parakeets and cockatoos of the Australian continent, of which 55 species are known to science. Australian birds were introduced into Europe only about 200 years ago. Some of these parakeets are now rare and in danger of extinction due to the encroachment of civilization. During this time the lories, and new species of cockatoos, parrots, and parakeets were discovered in many South Pacific islands. Many of these are extremely local species and deserve man's full protection.

Some psittacines extinct became so within the space of only a few hundred years. Some rare species are being bred in good numbers here and abroad by aviculturists who deserve much credit. The best method of preventing the extinction of birds would be to encourage aviculturists to breed and sell them. In their native lands, government protection should be given, and a specified number permitted to be trapped and sold to bird breeders and fanciers each year. Between natural and captive breeding, a species's continued existence would be ensured.

Taming

Psittacine birds are different from all other birds in that they have strong, hooked beaks and all have two toes behind and two in front. During their evolution, these birds came to prefer climbing to hopping from branch to branch. Species such as the hanging-parrots have a locking joint in their legs which enables them to hang from a branch and sleep upside down, their favorite position at night.

Before training a bird to talk, it is first necessary to tame it by winning its confidence and getting your presence and that of others acceptable to the bird. The larger psittacine birds become very tame and attached to their owners, especially when obtained at a young age, 2 to 6 months. When an older bird is purchased, more patience and understanding are required of the owner, particularly if the bird is very wild or has been mistreated or neglected. Full-grown parrots, macaws, and cockatoos can bite hard and should be approached slowly, without making any quick, sudden movements or loud noises. Offering a tidbit from the hand (not candy or cake) or scratching their heads gently are winning suggestions. Various nuts, hard-boiled egg yolk, celery stalk, a small piece of fresh corn on the cob, etc., make tempting offerings for the large psittacines.

Hunger, one of the strongest instincts, should not be overlooked as a good method to use in taming any animal. I soon tamed a mixed flock—ten finches and grass-parakeets flying about in a room—by withholding all seed for a couple of hours. I would then sit down with a large pan of seed on my lap and remain still. Before long, the boldest would fly down nearby and sidle over to the pan. Then, with a flurry of wings, the rest of the flock would follow suit. Soon there would be a bevy of jittery birds on my lap, busy filling their crops. With nervous glances at their surroundings, they would all fly off if I made the slightest move. I wouldn't advise this unless you have patience and an hour in which to relax with your birds.

Another way of taming a wild bird is to place the cage right beside you while reading, writing, or sewing. A nervous bird will eventually take your presence for granted. Birds kept singly tame more readily than those in the company of other birds. Some of the larger birds enjoy a little roughing up from their owner, as they like attention. This doesn't mean teasing, which would make a bird vicious. They do enjoy having their heads scratched and backs stroked. They will eventually expect this attention from persons they know who are near them. With the larger psittacines, a towel or glove should be used at first in handling them, till they get used to their master.

Examining Your Bird

I always believe in a thorough examination of all birds, going over them by hand once a month. Wings, tail, and body should be looked over, as there is always the possibility of finding some minor or

Tame Parrots

major condition in your pet which could be corrected. This may be an ingrown feather, claws or beak needing trimming, a swollen or dark abdomen indicating egg binding or liver trouble. The vent should also be examined. The legs, if rough and too scaly and encrusted with droppings, need washing with warm water, then anointing with either mineral oil, castor oil, or vaseline, to soften the scales and kill any scaly mites, if they are present.

You may find that your bird is plucking its pin feathers. Suggested remedies for bird disorders will be given later in this book. This is also the time, while looking your bird over, to apply the proper insecticide powder with a small rubber-bulb blower under the feathers close to the body where mites would be found. Even if your bird doesn't have any mites, a once-a-month delousing is a good preventative. This is best done in the evening, so that the powder will remain among the feather shafts overnight. In the morning, when the bird is uncovered, it is best to let it bathe in tepid water to remove most of the powder adhering to the feathers. If the bird won't bathe, it should be sprayed with lukewarm water to make it preen itself.

When handling untame larger psittacines for examination and necessary ministrations, two leather-gloved persons should handle the bird, one to hold the head and legs, and the other to look it over and hold the wings. Polly might object to this treatment, but it should be done for the bird's continued good health.

If a parrot has a long tail, in many cases it is called a "parakeet."

7

Teaching Parrots to Talk

Whichever species of bird is selected for training, it is preferable to buy young and, if possible, hand-raised birds between 2 and 6 months old. A bird's learning ability is less rapid the older it becomes. It is much more difficult to teach a wild or untrained adult bird, as its own calls or whistles will have been firmly implanted in its memory. However, a grown bird still can learn, but the owner will have to use more patience in teaching words to it.

There is much variation among individual birds in their ability to imitate the human voice, whether hand-raised or wild, young or adult. This faculty depends also on the species selected, the owner's teaching technique and patience, and most important, the tameness of the bird itself. Half the success is assured with a bird which is calm and gives you a bold look when you approach it. In talking ability, the Grey Parrot is said to be the most proficient among birds. However, by careful comparison, it seems that the Greater Indian Hill Mynah and the Javan Hill Mynah (which is larger) are more distinct in pronunciation, with more human tonal qualities than Grey or amazon parrots. Hill Mynahs don't seem to need as much prompting as parrots

do to start talking. They will answer words or whistles in a few seconds. Parrots, on the other hand, take longer to get started, and although their tonal qualities aren't as human, a parrot's memory is able to retain a greater vocabulary than the Hill Mynah.

The various species of amazon parrots from the American tropics are good talkers, some better than others. Cockatoos can also be taught to talk. Less proficient talkers are: macaws, cockatiels, conures, grass-parakeets, lovebirds, and the larger parakeet species.

To teach a bird to talk, constant repetition of a word or short phrase is necessary. This can be done at different times, such as before removing the cover from the cage in the morning. In the dark with no distractions, a bird will concentrate on listening and answering back. Repeating words at feeding time or when giving it a preferred tidbit helps also. At times, when you may be out of sight, you may hear your bird trying to enunciate some word or phrase. This is a good opportunity to repeat what you want it to learn. Or if the bird seems to be attempting a different expression from what you are teaching it, fit in words or a short phrase to go with the bird's vocal

Teaching Parrots to Talk

efforts and make them clear. Meanwhile, keep out of sight and don't approach the cage.

Still another excellent method of teaching your bird to talk, whistle, or sing a tune is by having a phonograph record or tape made with a few words or short phrase on it. If your own voice isn't clear and distinct, some friend of yours could oblige by repeating it into the recording machine for you. The clearest voice is that of a child, next a woman's, and lastly a man's. The recording should be played at different times during the day, and it will surely drill the lesson into your bird. Let's hope that you can stand hearing the sound of your own voice frequently. It is important when making a recording to limit it to a few words or a phrase only. If you change over to different words or sentences, your time and money are wasted. Birds have a small mental capacity and cannot assimilate too much at one time. If you wish to teach it more, make another recording. The second recording can have the previous lesson partly incorporated into it; however, emphasis should be placed on the new vocabulary. A criticism of some recordings sold is that they contain far too many words or sayings, which makes them worthless for teaching purposes. Therefore, to build up a good vocabulary in a bird through the use of recordings, have a new one made for each lesson. The previous sayings may be repeated in parts of each successive recording, till the last one contains everything the bird has been taught to say or whistle. Technology has made another task easier to accomplish.

The Grey Parrot.

Housing and Breeding

Psittacine birds may be kept on stands or confined in large-enough cages or outdoor aviaries. The size of all accommodations, of course, will depend on the size of the bird; some specifics are given in later chapters. Pet birds enjoy spending time out of their cages—and are more enjoyable then too. Stands should have wooden perches, the ends of which should have metal caps to protect them from the bird's gnawing. A block of wood or a piece of branch may be tied near the perch, as these birds all like to whittle away on something. This exercises their constantly growing bills, trimming them, and helps to prevent feather plucking.

An outdoor breeding aviary for the larger parakeets would have to be about 20 feet long by 6 feet wide by 6 feet high. For parrots and cockatoos, the length should be from 25 to 30 feet, for macaws a little longer. Six feet of the roof and sides of these aviaries should be solid, to act as a shelter from wind and rain, and to keep the food dry. When constructing a breeding enclosure, length is the most important consideration. Plenty of wing exercise and the proper food are necessary to keep them in top breeding condition and in good health. Perches should be placed only at each end of the enclosure with clearance from the sides for the tail. To compel the lazy larger psittacines to use their wings more often, it is advisable also to build a solid 2 or 3-foot wall from the ground, all around the cage, instead of using mesh in this part of the construction. Parrots, cockatoos, and macaws use their wings as little as possible in captivity, and this wall forces them to fly up or down to their food dish, rather than to crawl along the mesh. By attaching 1½ to 2-foot sheet-metal sections to the sides of the pen (thru the center of which you place your perch ends), Polly has to fly to get anywhere.

The site for the enclosure should be considered before any construction is done, and this should be in a sheltered spot, out of strong winds, drafts, or dampness. A southeast exposure is good, as birds like morning sun and bright quarters, especially in winter. In summer the aviary may be partly shielded from the sun's rays with vines. Some psittacines won't touch growing vegetation, but most will destroy it. In that case, color and shade may be created around your aviaries by growing attractive vines, such as the various species of morning glories, clematis,

Housing and Breeding

thunbergia, etc. In the South, bougainvillea, allamanda and many others are suitable. Kudzu vine, dutchman's pipe, and the ivies furnish dense shade but insignificant flowers. These vines may be trained over wire or string stretched and fastened a foot from the wire mesh to prevent their destruction by the birds.

A year-round outdoor aviary should consist of an enclosed, dry shelter which opens into a wire flight. The breeding enclosure with shelter previously described was a simple open type for use during mild weather or in the South. The dimensions for a year-round enclosure may be the same, with the shelter room 6 feet square. This should be constructed with tongue-and-groove boards, which will give a draft-proof wall. For snug insulation, the inside walls and ceiling may have a half-inch sheet of composition board, after which the whole interior should be whitewashed. Whitewashing should be done at the beginning and end of each breeding season to keep the place spic and span, free of mites and disease. Finishing the outside depends on how much you care to spend. The cheapest method is to paint or creosote the walls and tar-paper the roof. The outside may also be entirely tar-papered or, if you wish to make a neat, attractive building, you may use the many styles, designs, and colors of imitation-brick or shingle siding which are available.

Keeping Out Rats and Mice

If you build the solid 2 to 3-foot wall from the ground all around the outside flight, your birds will be protected from cats, rats, mice, and snakes above ground. However, you won't keep the enclosure free from intrusion with this wall only, as mice and rats burrow underground. It is necessary to dig a 1½-foot deep trench all around the outside flight. Quarter-inch wire mesh tarred or painted should be placed around the flight base 1½ feet into the ground. One edge of the mesh should be stapled along the base, or else embed this end in the cement flooring. A better method is to fasten the mesh with laths. The other end of the mesh should be bent at right angles away from the aviary and laid along the sides of the trench. The reason for bending it in this way is that a mouse, burrowing down the side of the aviary, is discouraged when it encounters the mesh leading away from the

11

Housing and Breeding

direction it wants to go. The specification of ¼-inch mesh is made because a very young mouse can actually go through the more commonly used ½-inch mesh. This has actually happened in aviaries. The baby mouse got in, but couldn't leave the same way, as its full tummy couldn't go through the ½-inch mesh. Many birds, even small ones, are not afraid of mice; however, their droppings may cause illness, and they will kill and eat nestlings. Thin galvanized or corrugated sheet-metal may be used instead of ¼-inch mesh.

Flooring

Another method of protection against underground-burrowing vermin, if you have earth or turf flooring, is to cover the whole enclosure floor with ¼-inch mesh a few inches under the soil. It will be too expensive to do this if you are building several breeding flights, and won't be necessary if you have desirable concrete flooring.

A floor of earth, even though turned over regularly, can be a breeding place for avian diseases which will wipe out your flock. The excreta of a sick bird remains in the soil. It is a fact that turkeys are so susceptible to disease that they are raised in pens well off the ground, unless they are on an open range. Turkeys are kept well away from the hardier chicken, and this should apply to cage birds also.

Concrete flooring should extend below the frost line, with an under-layer of gravel or cinders. In your locality, you may find out how much or how little you have to excavate so your cement floor won't heave or crack in cold weather. For easy cleaning and quick drying, a few drainage holes should be made around the enclosure, with ¼-inch mesh over them. At the spot where the holes lead into the ground, fill in a square-foot hole with stones for drainage. An occasional sprinkling of chlorinated-lime powder will keep this hole free from odors and germs.

Whether you are building one breeding enclosure or several, a quick and thorough cleaning of the flights may be facilitated through the following suggestions: The concrete floor may be graded in three ways to enable water, excreta, etc., to flow off freely, and to dry quickly. It may be either slanted slightly from a raised center down to the side drainage holes, or else the floor may be raised slightly on all sides, and graded to a depression in the center leading to a drainage hole. Still another method would be to raise the flooring in the rear and grade it down slightly to the front, where water will run into a channel leading to a drainage pit. Where a row of breeding flights are laid out, all the flooring may lead to a single channel for drainage. Using a hose either alone or with a broom, once or twice a week, is sufficient to keep such cement floors clean and quick-drying. You may also sprinkle sand or sawdust on the floor to absorb droppings.

Planting Greens in the Aviary

With most psittacine birds it is a waste of time to plant shrubbery in their aviary. Certain species of Australian parakeets, such as Bourke's, would never destroy plants, but most of them do. Psittacines do need greens, so it would be a good idea to make a two-foot-square space with wooden forms at the sunny end of the enclosure before setting the concrete floor. Plant mixed grass and grain seeds in this space, making a raised cement border all around, so it won't be flooded every time you hose down the floor. The birds will eat some of this growth, and when it's long enough and you spray it on a sunny morning, psittacines who don't bathe in a water bowl will greatly enjoy rolling in the wet grass.

Installing Wire Mesh

When building the flight sides, it is unnecessary to use the small ¼-inch mesh used for mouse-proofing underground. A larger suitable mesh may be ½-inch for small birds such as parrotlets, grass-parakeets, and lovebirds. For large parakeets, 1-inch mesh will suffice. A very heavy gauge 2 or 3-inch mesh will hold parrots, cockatoos, and macaws. The regular 2x4 studs may be used for framing the roof and sides. The mesh may be fastened to the wood framing with staples, or a better job can be done with battens, nailed down every foot. In this latter method, the mesh can be stretched better and looks better. The 2x4 studs should be placed on the corners and at about 6-foot intervals around the sides. The mesh used should be galvanized. It is not worthwhile to paint mesh, when you keep birds that are constantly clambering around, unless the wire is not rust-proof. Hot water, washing soda, and a scrub brush used occasionally on the mesh will keep it clean.

Housing and Breeding

Some psittacine birds, especially if closely related, will have fierce fights through the wires if one piece of mesh makes the wall for two flights. Although a single piece is more economical in constructing a row of breeding flights, it may be to the fancier's advantage to put up a separate piece of mesh for each flight, spaced 6 inches apart, which allows for cleaning feathers, leaves, etc., from between them.

Doors and Windows

A narrow, full-length door should be made between the shelter room and the flight. This may be left open all the time in mild weather and closed with the birds inside the shelter on cold nights. When open it permits the birds to fly the length of the whole enclosure.

At one corner of the flight, double doors should be installed for your entrance to the aviary. This is necessary to prevent the escape of the birds, which could otherwise get by you. Instead of making a porch for this purpose, space and material will be saved if you build a door at one corner. Inside at an angle install an inner door. A spring on the outside door will further make your enclosure escape-proof. The space between the doors can also be used as a trap for catching your birds.

Windows may be placed on the three sides of the shelter. If you wish, a window may be put in the wall separating the shelter from the flight. Glass, if used, should have mesh over it as the larger birds might go through. A better material in every way is plastic. It permits a greater percentage of the ultraviolet rays of the sun to penetrate. The 1/16-inch thickness is sufficient to hold your birds, so wire mesh over it is not required. This plastic has strong resiliency, and a bird will bounce back when flying against it, with less chance of having a broken neck than when flying against glass.

Nests

Hollow logs or large barrels make the most satisfactory nests for the larger psittacines. They may be hung upright or horizontally. Some birds prefer them to be hung in the open flight, while others prefer them inside the shelter. In the upright position, the eggs are less likely to roll around and get broken and chilled. When breeding the larger parakeets, it is better that pairs of a related species are not kept close together. Tame birds are not the best breeders; the wild ones breed the best.

Feeding Parrots

I don't know the circumstances under which you, the parrot fancier, live nor where, but the following wide variety of suitable foods for psittacines is listed so your bird may have a well-balanced and varied diet.

The staple diet of parrots, macaws, and cockatoos should consist of equal parts of seeds, greens, and fruits. The seed portion should be composed of the following: sunflower, hulled oats, canary seed, and large red or white millet. Other seeds may be added for variety, such as wheat (soaked overnight in water), cracked corn (dry or soaked), buckwheat, a small quantity of hemp seed and peanuts (raw). If you don't care to make your own seed mixture, "parrot seed" may be purchased ready-mixed in package form from any pet shop or supply house. A few of the large nuts (walnut, almond, brazil nut, cashew, hazel, etc.) may be supplied every day. The larger species can easily crack the hard shells, and this will keep them pleasantly occupied. Seeds do not contain all the elements required in a parrot's diet. Supply them daily with fresh greens such as beet tops, celery stalks, fresh peas in the pod, raw carrot, and uncooked corn on the cob.

A "year-round outdoor aviary," consisting of a completely enclosed shelter room, wire-mesh flight, and double doors.

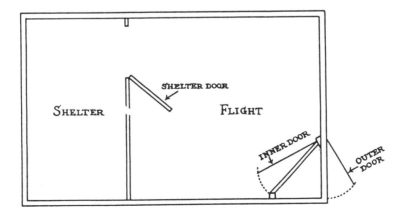

SHELTER

SHELTER DOOR

FLIGHT

INNER DOOR

OUTER DOOR

15

Feeding Parrots

No more than a third of a large psittacine bird's diet should consist of cut-up fruits, cherries, grapes, or berries. Citrus fruits may be given, but not too often, and only a few small pieces, as oranges do not agree too well with these birds and they, like all other birds, are able to synthesize their own vitamin-C requirements, not needing it in their food as we humans do. Another way in which we differ from them is that birds, dogs, and cats do not perspire, as they lack the sweat glands and pores that we have. They pant and we don't.

Cod-liver oil should be given in cold weather by letting 1 teaspoonful of the oil soak into 1 pint of seed overnight, mixing it in well. It may be given also by putting 3 or 4 drops every other day on soft food.

As a change in diet, beneficial treats may be supplied frequently, such as buttered whole-wheat bread or bread soaked in milk and squeezed dry. Other excellent items are grated hard-boiled egg yolk, dried dates or figs, a dry dog biscuit, brown or wild rice (paddy rice) boiled in milk or water, and sprouted seeds. Seeds will sprout if placed in a pan or box of damp peatmoss in the sun. When three inches tall, sections of this may be separated, thus furnishing fresh, tender, vitamin-filled greens.

On the above soft food, you could add a pinch of vitamin-mineral supplement every other day, especially during molting or when breeding.

Although it is always advisable to vary your parrot's diet for health and long life and to help prevent the bad habit of feather plucking, do not give it candy, cake (except fruit cake), coffee, beer, or table scraps.

Some fanciers, after experimenting, think that a little cooked meat is beneficial in supplying extra protein. This idea is worth trying. A mineral block is beneficial also and will help keep your bird out of mischief too.

Photographs on pages 17-24: 17—Blue-fronted Amazon (Amazona aestiva). *18—Blue and Yellow Macaw* (Ara ararauna). *19—Hyacinth Macaw* (Anodorhynchus hyacinthinus). *20—Turquoise Parrot* (Neophema pulchella). *22—Malabar Parakeet* (Psittacula columboides). *23—Regent Parrot* (Polytelis anthropeplus). *24—Grey Parrot* (Psittacus erithacus).

17

Parrots

Grey parrot (*Psittacus erithacus erithacus*). This species, one of the best known parrots, is said to be the best talker among psittacine birds. In the United States, they have always been very popular.

The different subspecies of Greys inhabit the Congo region, Gold Coast, and throughout western and central Africa. One place where Grey Parrots were found particularly abundant was on Prince's Island off the Gold Coast. On this island there is a 1200-foot mountain called Pico de Papagaio ("Peak of the Parrot") which, although not very high as mountains go, is covered with a dense forest of trees of great size on its slopes. It is difficult to penetrate this forest due to the masses of lianas and other jungle growth. At sunset, great numbers of Greys fly in from the lowlands where they feed and roost for the night in the security of the mountain's jungle. There are other mountains on Prince's Island, but this one is the preferred location for night roosting and for raising the young in the breeding season.

Most fanciers don't know it, but Greys differ in size and in coloring. Size may vary from 12 to 15¾ inches, depending upon subspecies, age, and sex. Some have red feathers in the wings, others have many red feathers mixed throughout the gray body feathers. Still others have pink feathers mixed in the gray plumage. There are even partial albinos, albinos with red tails and, very rarely, completely white birds, and gray ones with white tails instead of the normal scarlet.

Description: Cock: Body pearl gray, having the feathers of the head, neck, and abdomen margined with whitish gray. Tail scarlet, square and short. Bill is black. Skin patch around the eyes, lores, and above bill grayish white. Feet grayish with black claws. Eyes with a clear yellow iris. Hen: Similar to the cock but smaller, with shorter neck and smaller, rounder head. To tell the sexes apart, look at the bare skin at the back of the eye, which you will find to be less extensive, more rounded, and less elliptical in shape in the hen than in the cock. She is a darker shade of gray, and the light edgings of the feathers are less distinct than those of the cock. A look at the head also helps to differentiate the sexes. The cock's head is more arched, longer, with a smaller bill having more of a hook than the hen's. She has a broader, flatter head, with a stouter bill, thicker at the base than the cock's. By carefully comparing the above differences, you will be able to

Parrots

determine the sex of your birds, as they are otherwise very similar.

Immature birds have the tail dark red at the tips, and the under tail coverts dark red tinged with gray. Young birds may be easily ascertained by the eye coloring, which is first black or very dark grayish in a very young bird, changing in five to six months to light gray, and at one year of age to a clear yellow. At full maturity, 3½ to 4 years, the irises are clear yellowish white. In a young bird, the cheeks and forehead are not as light colored as in the adults.

Complete instructions for feeding in captivity are given in a previous chapter applying to all parrots. It is interesting to the fancier, however, to know what Greys feed on in the wild. These parrots, like crows and many other birds, go out foraging during the day to preferred feeding grounds, and at dusk wing their way back to favorite roosting trees for the night. In the wild, their food preference is given to palm nuts which they can easily crack, then various grains, especially maize. Wild fruits form part of their diet also.

Breeding: Greys require a breeding flight 25 to 30 feet long, by 6 to 8 feet wide and high. Length is the most important dimension. More explicit details on properly building an enclosure are given in a previous chapter. Both parents take turns in incubating and feeding the young. While one parent is sitting on the eggs, the other will come up and feed it. In the wild, Grey Parrots nest in colonies, one tree having two or more families in its hollow limbs or trunk, which are used year after year. In captivity, no more than one pair should be bred in an enclosure. The young will be cared for by the parents for quite some weeks, but if they show signs of wanting to nest again, remove the young.

It may be necessary to feed your young parrot by hand, in which case an inexpensive mixture of the following may be made up: chicken or turkey growing mash—5 lbs.; dried buttermilk or whey—1 lb.; oatmeal or Pablum—2 lbs. Two or three drops of cod-liver oil should be given in the food per day. If available, you may add to the above a pound of any of the following: alfalfa meal; dried egg; whole-milk powder; pea or bean meal; grated hard-boiled egg; and raw carrot. When the young are older, whether hand-fed or not, they may be weaned from soft food by giving them seeds (parrot mix) which were soaked overnight in water, and eventually they will eat the seeds dry.

Parrots have the unusual ability of being able to retain their breeding condition even though kept for years on a stand or in a cage. One peculiarity about parrots so kept is that it requires some time for the bird to fully recover the use of its wings when placed in a 25 to 30-foot breeding pen.

As family pets, Grey Parrots may be recommended for their docility, gentleness, and wonderful talking powers. You and your friends will be well entertained with unexpected remarks from its gift of gab. They are easy to care for like the amazon parrots, also live over 50 years (some reaching 80 to 100), and will be a companion to you if you are alone. A bird may even outlive you, and they have often been willed to another generation as a family heirloom. Greys, together with the Panama Yellow-crowned Amazon and the Yellow-headed Amazon, are the best talkers among parrots.

The Timneth Grey Parrot (*Psittacus erithacus timneh*) is a distinct subspecies of the Grey Parrot, and is smaller and darker gray; size, 12 inches. The body above is dark gray, abdomen and rump light gray. Tail dark red. Bill pale yellow at the base, black towards the tip. Its range is farther north in West Africa than the nominate subspecies, and includes Liberia and lower Sierra Leone.

Amazon Parrots

Amazon parrots are exclusively tropical American birds, and all have the ability to repeat words, whistles, and sounds. They are easy to care for, hardy and affectionate. Their lifespan is well over 50 years. Among the many species, the best talkers are:

Yellow-headed Amazon (*Amazona oratrix*). Range: Mexico to British Honduras. 15 inches. This gentle and affectionate bird is said to be the best talker among the amazons. The body is a lovely shade of green, and when fully mature (at 3 years old), the entire head and upper neck are yellow. There are a few red spots on shoulders and wings. Young birds have only a small amount of yellow in the front part of the head, which increases in area up to 3 years of age; it spreads very gradually and slowly.

Yellow-crowned Amazon (*Amazona o. ochrocephala*). Range: Northern South America. This species, all green with a yellow forehead and dark bill, makes a nice talker.

Parrots

Panama Yellow-crowned Amazon (*Amazona o. panamensis*). Range: Panama to Colombia. 15 inches. Similar to the preceding, with a paler green body and yellow forehead. The bill in this subspecies is white. Said to be the second-best talker among Amazons.

Blue-fronted Amazon (*Amazona aestiva*). Range: Brazil. This species has the same nice shade of green as the others, but it has a blue forehead, yellow throat and cheeks. The patch on the wings is scarlet, and the bill is black.

Cuban Amazon (*Amazona leucocephala*). Range: Cuba and Isle of Pines. 10 to 11 inches. This species is one of the most beautiful amazons. The body is green, with white forehead, red throat and cheeks. The wings and tail have feathers of blue, red, and green. This parrot, though prettier than the others, is not as good a talker.

I wish to mention an extremely desirable amazon with friendly ways and which makes a nice talker. It is a smaller bird, about 10½ inches. It is the **White-fronted Amazon** (*Amazona albifrons*). Range: Western Mexico, Yucatan, Guatemala, Nicaragua, and Costa Rica. This small parrot is striking in that it has a scarlet circle around the eyes, scarlet patch on the wings, and a blue crown and breast. I've seen these birds, and think they make a fine, colorful pet for the small home or apartment.

Caiques

Caiques are small, stout birds of the parrot family, with unusually striking coloration. Hand-reared specimens are comical in their actions, and show aggressive tendencies towards each other. They have a short tail with pointed feathers which is less than half the length of the wings. Sexes are alike. Their range lies in northeastern South America. They are kept as pets in that area, but are not generally so well known in the United States, except in zoological gardens. The two species are:

Black-headed Caique (*Pionites melanocephala*). Body green; head black with a patch of green in front and below eyes. The nape is orange, cheeks and throat are yellow, the breast is white. The bill, feet, and naked skin around the eyes is black. The iris of the eye has an inner ring brown, and an outer one red.

White-bellied Caique (*Pionites leucogaster*). Body green, white below, with orange crown.

Parrotlets

P arrotlets are really miniatures of the large amazon parrots. They are not quite as small as the pygmy-parrots of the South Pacific islands, but are from about 4 to 5½ inches in length, which makes them quite small. They are slow-moving except when flying, when they are swift on the wing with an undulating flight. Parrotlets are bright green, some having bright shades of blue on the wings, under wing coverts, and the rump, in cocks only. Hens are plain bright green having mostly yellow foreheads. Thus the sexes are easy to distinguish.

They may be kept with the smallest finches, providing the flight is roomy. One pair may be kept in an ordinary canary cage. These little birds are never noisy or objectionable, their common call being a pleasant *peet-peet* repeated in staccato fashion when feeling happy and exuberant. When handled against their will, they utter a rasping sound.

A remarkable trait is their extreme attachment to one another when in pairs, and even two cocks kept together were observed to copulate. If separated in the same room, they will call their *peet-peet* back and forth continually till united. These little birds like to stay in one place for long periods of time, especially if kept in a small cage by themselves. If one is handled often enough, it will eventually become finger-tame, though never a talker. They are similar in appearance to lovebirds, having very short tails, with the central two tail feathers the longest.

The range of parrotlets is from Mexico through Central and northern South America to Brazil and Bolivia. The distribution of blue on the wings and rump separates the species.

Feeding and Care

The main diet for parrotlets is the standard parakeet mixture, with a teaspoonful of cod-liver oil mixed in one pint of seed. It is difficult to induce these birds to eat greens, although some do eat dandelion, but they will greatly relish fresh corn on the cob or a piece of sweet apple. If they do not take to these other foods at first, just remove all seed for half a day.

Parrotlets, in common with other psittacine birds, do like something to chew on, and should be provided with sections of bark or pieces of soft wood. There is some indication that they like raw hamburger, as they have been known to eat the heads of birds that died of natural causes in their aviaries.

In winter, if fresh corn is not available, they can be given cracked dry corn in a separate dish from their parakeet mixture. Some parrotlets may eat the smaller sunflower seeds, and this should be encouraged by at first removing other seeds and giving just sunflower in a separate dish.

Parrotlets will not bathe, but prefer to roll in wet grass, lettuce, or cabbage leaves. It is here suggested to spray them every week or two with tepid water or to give them a quick dip in lukewarm water. Place them in direct sun afterwards to dry out and preen. This will bring out the bright green of their plumage.

Breeding

Parrotlets lay up to 6 eggs in a clutch, with two nests per season. A Budgie nest box with a concave block at the bottom is most suitable, as they do not build nests. A very thin sprinkling of peatmoss may be placed in the concave to lessen any danger of egg breakage. The young are fed regurgitated seed, and the parents should also be provided with fresh corn on the cob if available and, if they will take it, whole-wheat bread and greens. Ground oystershell should have been provided two months prior to breeding. Newly paired parrotlets will be encouraged to breed if other parrotlets are kept in adjoining breeding compartments, or even Budgerigars. The breeding pair should be given strict solitude except when being fed and watered.

An amusing characteristic of Spengel's Blue-wing especially is a rattling sound of irritation uttered by the cocks against the more active members of their aviary in disapproval of any clumsiness displayed in flight.

Blue-winged Parrotlet *(Forpus xanthopterygius)*. Range: Guianas and eastern Brazil. This is the smallest species, being little over 4 inches. Their body is bright green, including the rump. The cocks have light blue on the wings, with royal blue on the under wing coverts. The hen has a yellow forehead.

Green-rumped Parrotlet *(Forpus passerinus viridissimus)*. Range: Venezuela. Bright green with only a trace of blue on the cock's rump.

Another very pretty species is the **Spectacled Parrotlet** *(Forpus conspicillatus)*. Range: Panama to Colombia.

Lovebirds

Lovebirds are small birds of the parrot family, barely exceeding 6 inches in length, with stout bills and short, square tails. Pairs are affectionate, and although some people believe that the death of one of a pair will cause the other to pine away, this is not true. A new mate will be just as acceptable as the old. Even though pairs show affection to each other, this does not prevent them from being quarrelsome at times with other species as well as with their own kind, especially while nesting or when too many are confined in too small a cage. Lovebirds should not be kept with birds smaller than themselves, such as finches, as it is easy for them to break a leg or a wing of weaker birds. They take good care of themselves in mixed company, and can hold their own against much larger birds.

All lovebirds —genus *Agapornis*— are inhabitants of Africa and a few adjacent islands, such as Madagascar. Nine species are at present known to avicultural science, and although some have a very wide distribution, others are extremely local. Their lifespan is from 8 to 10 years. The name "lovebird" is sometimes erroneously given to the Budgerigar, which is smaller, with a long pointed tail—an entirely different genus. There are still other small parrots wrongly called lovebirds which come from South America; they are properly known as parrotlets, and are of still another genus.

Sexing: In some species of lovebirds, the sexes look alike; in others the hen differs from the cock and is easily told apart. With species that look alike, the best method to distinguish sex is to hold two birds firmly in each hand. When looking down on them, the head of the cock will be observed to be wider across between the eyes than that of the hen. The head of the female also appears to be more elongated.

The nine lovebird species can be divided into two groups: one with a distinct white eye ring, and the other without.

With Bare White Eye Ring: Fischer's Lovebird, *Agapornis fischeri;* Masked Lovebird, *Agapornis personata;* Black-cheeked Lovebird, *Agapornis nigrigenis;* Nyasa Lovebird, *Agapornis lilianae.*

Without Bare White Eye Ring: Peach-faced Lovebird, *Agapornis roseicollis;* Black-winged Lovebird, *Agapornis taranta;* Red-faced Lovebird, *Agapornis pullaria;* Black-collared Lovebird, *Agapornis swinderniana;* Grey-headed Lovebird, *Agapornis cana.*

Lovebirds

Nesting

Lovebirds like to build elaborate nests with straw, small twigs, and fresh bark which they strip off branches, etc., in a hollow log or a nest box, which should be 12 inches high, 6 inches wide, and 6 inches deep, with an entrance hole 2 inches in diameter near the top of the box. They are one of the few species of parrots that construct a nest in their nest box or hole in a tree trunk in the wild. While in the nest, the hen passes pieces of straw or strips of bark back and forth between her mandibles till they are soft and pliable. She fills the nest box full of this material, and then makes a curved entrance down to the bottom of the box, where the clutch of 4 to 7 eggs is laid. These are all-white and slightly oblong.

The incubation period for lovebirds is from 18 to 24 days, depending on the species. It requires 4 to 5 weeks for the young to leave the nest. They will go to nest any month of the year. However, because of the danger from egg binding in the hens during cold weather, it is best to start all species of lovebirds breeding late in March or early April, which will allow them to raise two or three nests of young by the end of October, when the nest boxes should be removed. During the cold months, they should be permitted to fly and recuperate from their breeding efforts. After taking down the nest boxes, thoroughly wash them out with hot water and strong soap. Almost all the various species of lovebirds will interbreed when permitted. The crosses produce some pretty hybrids which are usually fertile. This policy is not advised, however, as all are very similar in appearance. Fanciers want purebred birds of a definite species.

Young lovebirds should not be permitted to nest till at least 9 months old or, better yet, one year old. The breeding season in South Africa is different from ours. Their spring corresponds to our fall. With lovebirds hatched in June or July, it is very doubtful that they will breed in that fall or even the following spring. It will require the second fall season in September for them to start. Many persons buy lovebirds in the summer and want to breed them right away. This is mentioned so the prospective breeder will not blame the seller if his birds do not breed that year. They should be one year old for full sexual maturity.

Lovebirds

Feeding

All lovebirds require the same diet, consisting of equal parts of sunflower seed, canary seed, large millet, and oat or buckwheat groats; spray millet can be supplied for a change. Another inexpensive and very nourishing food supplied along with the regular seed diet, but in a separate dish, is an all-in-one chicken laying mash. Bird sand and crushed oystershell have to be given also.

Fresh greens can consist of lettuce, sprouted oats, dandelion, chickweed, etc. A little fruit can be given, such as halved orange, apple, or pear stuck on perch holders. An occasional treat for them, cut up in a dish, are cherries, grapes, and berries. During the breeding period, and once a week in winter, cod-liver oil can be given at the rate of 1 teaspoonful mixed in a pint of seed. No greater amount of cod-liver oil than that should be offered, or the birds will run the risk of diarrhea. Also, for feeding young, a slice of whole-wheat bread soaked in fresh milk and squeezed dry, with a pinch of vitamin-mineral food supplement (obtainable in a pet shop) is very beneficial. The slice of bread should not be left in the cage all day in hot weather. Sometimes a far ḻ..ṛ's

lovebirds may suffer a vitamin-D deficiency and go light; they hang on the cage wire with their bills and can fly but can't walk, just scuttling along on their chests. These afflicted birds recover the use of their legs if given cod-liver oil and hemp seed mixed into their regular mixture.

Housing

These birds should be kept in a cage where they can do some flying, at least 3 feet long, 20 inches wide, and 18 inches high. When kept in smaller cages, they just sit on the perch side by side, taking very little interest in their surroundings. In a large-enough cage or aviary, they are very active and amusing in their antics. Their full beauty is only noticed when in flight.

Three-quarter-inch wooden perches are suitable, but to keep them happily occupied and their beaks in trim, a branch from a nonpoisonous tree (such as fruit trees, willows, etc.) attached in their enclosure, will be appreciated.

Although an odd bird may bathe in a shallow dish, all are very fond of rolling and playing in wet grass or lettuce as Budgerigars do.

Lovebirds

Peach-faced Lovebird
(Agapornis roseicollis). Range: Southwest Africa. Body bright green, face and breast peach color. Bill flesh color. Rump bright blue, tail green with pink and blue markings. Female similar, but colors slightly duller.

This is the largest of the lovebirds, and resembles the Red-faced Lovebird; it is twice the size of the Nyasa. They are excellent breeders, and should be supplied with a slightly larger nest box than the others. The entrance hole should be about 2½ inches in diameter. There is no white eye ring in this species.

Because Peach-faced are such reliable breeders, more color varieties have been developed in this species than in any other. Yellow, Blue, Lutino, Pied, Cinnamon, and Dark are the most common of the primary factors, and many more varieties have been produced through various collocations of these.

Masked Lovebird *(Agapornis personata).* Range: Tanzania, Africa. Body green, paler on abdomen. Entire head black with a brownish tinge. Yellow breast and collar behind neck. Bill red. In this species the female is somewhat larger than the male, and of the same coloring.

Both have large bare white eye rings.

A variety has been developed by aviculturists, with a bluish head and distinct white eye rings; an attractive mutation now well established is called the Blue Masked Lovebird.

The Masked are one of the hardiest lovebirds for an outdoor aviary and are free breeders. The young emerge from the nest fully feathered, and in a few days they are hard to distinguish from the adults. Size, 1½ times that of the Budgerigar.

Fischer's Lovebird *(Agapornis fischeri).* Range: Tanzania, Africa. Body bright green. Orange red on forehead, paler orange on cheeks and throat. Olive green on head and neck. Rump, blue; bill, red. They also have a bare white eye ring. Sexes are alike. The Fischer's is 25% larger than the Nyasa. They are gregarious and happy when kept in flocks rather than in single pairs. This bird species first became known to aviculture in 1926. They are free breeders.

Black-cheeked Lovebird *(Agapornis nigrigenis).* Range: Zambia, Africa. Body green; forehead brown, merging into olive green at back of head. Cheeks and throat blackish, with a small patch of orange on upper breast; bill red. An attractive point is the distinct white eye ring on the dark head. The female is the same; however, sex can be determined by examining the eyes, which are different in males and females. These are one of the smallest lovebirds, being the same size as the Nyasa. They are free breeders, laying 4 to 6 eggs.

Grey-headed Lovebird

(*Agapornis cana*). Range: Madagascar. Male: Body, green; head, neck, and upper breast, lavender gray. Tail, green barred with black in both sexes. Bill horn color. The hen is all green. This species does not have an eye ring. This lovebird is not as hardy as the others. They are quarrelsome when kept with other birds, and are not too easy to breed. Size about that of the Nyasa.

Nyasa Lovebird (*Agapornis lilianae*).

Range: Nyasaland from Zambesi to the Loanga Valley, Africa. Body bright green. Top and sides of head, cheeks, and throat bright reddish orange. Back of head and neck olive. Bill red. The hen is similar but duller in coloring. This smallest lovebird has a bare white eye ring and is the least quarrelsome. Size, 1¼ times that of the Budgerigar.

Black-winged Lovebird

(*Agapornis taranta*). Range: Ethiopia. Male: bright green, with a scarlet forehead and bill. Female: all green, and does not have a red forehead. There is no white eye ring in this species. They are hardy, but difficult to breed unless aviary conditions are just right for them. Size about 25% larger than the Nyasa. They are very scarce in the United States.

Red-faced Lovebird (*Agapornis pullaria*).

Range: Equatorial Africa. Body bright green. Red orange forehead, face, and bill. Short tail banded with red and black. Female: face more orange, and the under wing coverts are green, while on the male they are black. There is no white eye ring in this species.

These lovebirds are delicate when first imported, but very hardy when acclimated. By purchasing them in early summer, they will have a chance to get acclimated if they are to be kept outdoors during cold weather. These birds get along well in a mixed collection, but are difficult to breed in confinement.

Macaws

These are New World birds only, inhabitants of South and Central America. The large forms are the biggest psittacine birds in the world, at least in length, some measuring 3 feet, though the Kea of New Zealand is more massive in breadth. The average person doesn't know that there are a number of green species much smaller in size than the ones commonly known; several all-blue species exist also.

Macaws may be kept just as pets, or they may be bred in captivity in the manner of other parrots. In the wild they nest in hollow tree trunks or holes in large branches, enlarging the hole with their powerful bills. The same site is used for years. The big species lay two large roundish eggs in a clutch, while the smaller species lay 3 to 4. When brooding, the long tail projects from the nesting hole. Their eggs are the size of a chicken's, but rounder. Both cock and hen take turns at incubating, and there are usually two broods per year. Macaws are conspicuous in flight, as they usually fly high and in pairs, screaming as they go. They may easily be heard a mile away.

Macaws are sly in the wild. When they plunder a ripening corn field, they post sentinels in the surrounding trees. Their usual loud calls are stilled while feeding unless danger approaches. If that happens, the sentinel gives loud calls, and the whole flock rises and heads for the nearest woods.

Macaws make docile pets and, like parrots and cockatoos, enjoy having their heads scratched. Naturally they should never be teased, or you will make them vicious. Some macaws make nice talkers, but most of them just say a few words or short sentences. You have to obtain them very young for tutoring.

Because of the long tail, they are best kept tethered to a stand instead of in a small cage. The stand should be very strong, with the perch ends capped with metal to withstand the bird's powerful bill. A block of wood or thick piece of a branch should be fastened to the stand with a length of small linked chain so the bird may exercise its bill in playing with it, instead of destroying its perch. If you are able to supply your macaw with a large wired flight 40 feet or more in length during the summer months, it will obtain some much-needed exercise. Macaws, parrots, and cockatoos that do not usually have much opportunity for flying exercise in captivity require some time to recover full use of their wings if placed in a large flight after having been kept more closely confined. They may be compelled to use their wings in a large flight by installing only two perches, one at each end. At each place where the perches are fastened, attach a three-foot diameter sheet-metal disk to the sides of the cage; the ends of each perch should be inserted in the exact center of each disk. This prevents your psittacine from clambering along the wire from the perch to the ground to feed. A similar treatment should be given to the bottom by erecting a solid 2- or 3-foot wall all around the sides. Your bird won't have any other choice left but to get its exercise by flying, if it is going to move anyplace.

Macaws in the genus *Ara* are differentiated from the blue kinds by having a complete bony ring in the skull around the eyes, and in all of them, the lores and cheek areas are devoid of feathers.

Scarlet Macaw *(Ara macao)*. Range: Mexico to Brazil. Introduced in Hawaii. 36 inches. Mostly scarlet with blue, red, and yellow on the wings. Four middle tail feathers are scarlet, the outer ones blue. Lower back and rump cobalt blue. Upper mandible white with black tip and edges. Lower mandible and feet black. Iris yellowish white and naked skin cheeks, light yellow.

Sexes alike.

Blue-and-Yellow Macaw *(Ara ararauna)*. Range: Panama to Paraguay. Head, back, wings and tail blue; abdomen orange yellow. Sexes alike but cock is larger; 36 inches.

Military Macaw *(Ara militaris)*. Range: Mexico to Peru and Bolivia. This species is 27 inches long and is mainly green with a scarlet forehead. Lower back and upper tail coverts bright blue. The four middle feathers of the tail are brownish red, tipped with blue.

Hyacinth Macaw *(Anodorhynchus hyacinthus)*. Range: Central Brazil. This is the largest blue macaw. Length is from 34 to 36 inches, about 20 being the tail. It is uniformly cobalt blue in body. Under surface of tail, wings, and entire bill black. Naked skin around eyes and around base of lower mandible bright yellow. This macaw is different from others in that it doesn't have a large bare skin area around the face. It is one of the scarcer macaws and inhabits dense tropical forests. Instead of building a nest in a tree, it is said to scoop out a burrow in the bank of a river, laying two eggs. Two broods are raised in a season. In the wild, these birds feed mainly on hard palm nuts. They are not a pet for the

Conures

home, as they are noisy, but would be suitable in a home with surrounding acreage.

Lear's Macaw *(Anodorhynchus leari)*. Range: Brazil. This second all-blue macaw is similar to the above but smaller, with head and breast duller blue.

Glaucous Macaw *(Anodorhynchus glaucus)*. Range: Southern Brazil, Paraguay, and Uruguay. This blue species is still smaller, but grayer in coloring.

There are smaller macaws more suitable for keeping in a small house or apartment.

Chestnut-fronted Macaws *(Ara severa)* are about the size of a parrot, 12 to 15 inches. They are mostly green with blue on the head, and under wing coverts scarlet. They are nice talkers.

Red-shouldered Macaw *(Ara nobilis)*. Range: Northern South America. One of the smallest macaws, 12 inches. Body, green; forehead, blue; under wing coverts and shoulder (mantle) scarlet.

Conures are close relatives of the macaws, with pointed faces like them, but feathered. Their coloring comprises bright yellow, red, and green. They are very hardy in captivity, and when acclimated may be kept in an outdoor aviary the year round. There are sometimes slight differences in coloring between the sexes. Conures don't make too good talkers, but are very affectionate. The natives in their homelands often keep them as pets. There are about 40 species ranging from Mexico through Central America to South America. These birds make some of the nicest tame psittacine bird pets possible for the small home, apartment, or even the bird lover in a furnished room. They become very much attached to their owner, and learn to say a few words, the Brown-throated Conure being especially affectionate.

It is after being away all day, or when just greeting your Conure in the morning that the bird's pleasure with your attention will be shown. They will learn a wolf whistle. When excited, the pupil of the eye will open and contract as the bird talks and whistles. This action of the pupil when excited is common among most of the larger psittacines.

In breeding, they should be given

the same nesting accommodations as those stated for other larger parakeets. Three to four eggs are laid in a clutch.

Feeding

Conures require a mixture of canary, large millets, hulled oats, and some buckwheat. Large sunflower seed should be given in a separate dish and, at times in winter, cracked corn. Like most psittacines of their size, they like fruit such as apple, grapes, bananas, etc., but little or no orange. The best green to give them is a halved fresh corn on the cob. A few drops of cod-liver oil should be added on the fruit or mixed in the canary-millet mixture at the rate of 1 teaspoonful to 1 pint of seed, and given in cold weather.

Some conures will enjoy bathing in an 8-inch flowerpot saucer. Those that don't should be sprayed with tepid water to bring out the bright green sheen of their plumage.

Brown-throated Conure *(Aratinga pertinax aeruginosa)* Range: Colombia and Venezuela. This species has dull blue over half its head, body light green, yellowish on abdomen and undertail feathers; blue flight feathers, black bill, and speckled brown throat. The sexes are almost indistinguishable, although cocks have a slightly longer and more massive head and bill and can be especially differentiated by a wider and more elliptical white skin patch around the eyes, which have a thin ringlet of small yellow feathers. Immatures in their first plumage have much speckled brown in their green plumage, especially on the abdomen, with the green very dark.

Even hens will act very affectionately toward each other, so it is difficult to tell them apart by their actions alone. By first training them to climb on an outstretched stick, they will trust you enough to eventually go on your finger.

Golden Conure *(Aratinga guarouba)*. Range: Northeast Brazil. This beautiful bird is almost all deep lemon yellow. The wing coverts are green, flights dark green above, golden olive below. It requires up to three years for this bird to acquire its full-adult golden plumage.

Peach-fronted Conure *(Aratinga aurea)*. Range: Guianas, Brazil, Bolivia, and Paraguay. Body mostly grass green, forehead, crown, and face orange. Lores and back of head, dull blue; abdomen, orange yellow. Bill is black, feet brownish, iris

Cockatoos

green to brown.

White-eared Conure *(Pyrrhura leucotis)*. Range: Eastern Brazil. This may be the prettiest and most elegant of the conures. It is mostly green, top of head and nape brownish black. Forehead, cheeks, shoulders, rump, tail tip, and middle of abdomen deep red. It inhabits the wooded coast region; they are said to be quite common, and to have bred in captivity.

Brotogeris Parakeets

This is a genus of small, green parakeets widely kept as pets. They are smaller than amazons and most conures. In all species, the sexes are alike. They are not very good talkers, but they do get used to a cage. Some of the seven species are:

Orange-chinned Parakeet *(Brotogeris jugularis)*. Range: Mexico to Colombia. Green with orange spot on chin.

Canary-winged Parakeet *(Brotogeris versicolorus)*. Range: South America. Body green with a patch of yellow on the wings.

Grey-cheeked Parakeet *(Brotogeris pyrrhopterus)*. Range: Ecuador and Peru. Body green, cheeks and throat pale gray, under wing coverts orange.

These birds are of the order Psittaciformes, subfamily Cacatuinae. Their range is confined to Australasia, as far east as the Solomon Islands, north to the Philippines, and west to the Celebes and Lombok.

Most cockatoos are white, although some are gray, brown, or black. They represent an advance in the evolution of parrots and are seemingly more intelligent. Some species make good talkers when tame and taught young, although in this respect they don't equal the Hill Mynah, Grey, and large amazon parrots. Methods of training them to talk are given in the first part of this book. They learn tricks more readily than these other birds. The all-white and rosy white species of cockatoos are about 12 in number.

Cockatoos have feathers which other birds don't have. These are fine, waxy filaments, on the body and under the wings, which break into a fine waxy powder when the bird preens itself. This is what helps it to retain the snow white plumage which is so much admired, as this powder is thus distributed throughout its feathers. It appears also that this waxy powder makes the feathers water repellent. If out in the rain, it is usually the tail feathers and wing tips only that

Cockatoos

get wet.

Cockatoos, especially the larger ones such as the Sulphur-crested, live to a more venerable age than even the proverbially long-lived parrot. It may reach 100 years, which makes it the longest-lived of all birds. Naturally, this depends on the good general care it receives. These are mostly large birds suitable for large enclosures in bird collections. The smaller ones make nice house pets and are very exotic-looking.

Cockatoos do better on stands or large cages than confined in a small cage. An outdoor aviary with shelter and flight is better yet. If kept in a cage in the house, their cage should be 4 feet long, 3 feet wide, by 3 feet high. A stand with the ends of the perch metal-covered would take up less room. Incidentally, these birds may be acclimated to remain outdoors the year round, being thickly feathered. If kept on a stand, or in a cage or aviary, supply them with a block of wood or a branch of a nonpoisonous tree to keep them occupied and to exercise their strong bills on. This will also help prevent the bad habit of feather plucking.

Breeding

These beautiful birds are well worth breeding, and require the same type and construction of breeding enclosure as that given previously for parrots. The dimensions should be larger than for parrots, especially for the larger species. This would be 30 feet long, by 8 feet high, by 8 feet wide. Perches should be large and placed only at either end of the enclosure to compel flight, as these birds are as lazy as parrots in this respect. Both sexes usually share in incubation. A suitable nest easy to obtain would be a large barrel. Cut a hole near the top of it, just large enough for them to enter, and inside the barrel, from the hole to the bottom, install a strip of 1-inch wire mesh. The floor of the barrel should be concave in the center to prevent the eggs rolling to the sides. To accomplish this, put in a layer of twigs or wood chips, or a section of turf upside down, making a hollow. A large branch should be attached to or near the nest box.

Two to three eggs form the clutch, and the incubation period lasts about a month, depending on size of bird and the species. The young remain in the nest about two months. When breeding, the parents should have solitude and be disturbed as little as possible. It will be a proud day for you to have

Cockatoos

succeeded in breeding a cockatoo.

Some of the better-known and more available species are here described:

Major Mitchell's Cockatoo (*Cacatua leadbeateri*). Range: Northwestern, western, and South Australia, and in the interior of Victoria, New South Wales, and Queensland. Size, 19 inches. It is the least plentiful of Australia's 11 species of cockatoos, scarce in many parts of its wide range, although appearing to increase in other areas, especially Wyperfeld National Park, Victoria, a wildlife sanctuary. This is one of the most beautiful and friendly of the larger cockatoos. The head, neck, and underparts are of a lovely shade of pink. The back, wings, and tail are snow-white. It has a wonderful crest which is lowered when the bird is resting, but when active, excited, or just feeling happy, is very strikingly elevated. It consists of a double row of feathers rose red at the base, followed by a broad band of yellow; running across this is a band of bright red, with white tips. This bird is an excellent mimic and whistler, although expensive. In the wild, it feeds on bulbous roots, and plant and grass seeds. The breeding season in Australia is from September to November, when 3 or

4 white eggs are laid in tree holes.

Sulphur-crested Cockatoo (*Cacatua galerita*). Range: Australia (except Western Australia, south of the Fitzroy River), King Island, and Tasmania. Other forms of this species occur in New Guinea, the Lesser Sunda Group, Moluccan Islands, and Solomon Islands. Introduced in Hawaii and in New Zealand. Size, 20 inches. Body snow-white, bill black, vent and underside of tail feathers yellow. Yellow pointed erectile crest. This is one of the best-known species. They are docile, more intelligent than a parrot, one of the best talkers among cockatoos, and widely kept as pets in Australia.

After a century of persecution by farmers whose wheat fields they raid, they still are as abundant today as they were before Australia's discovery. This is because these very intelligent birds know the danger of a man with a gun. When raiding a wheat field, they are shrewd enough to post sentinels which give warning to the feeding flock with shrill cries. These canny birds, like Master Crow, are usually out of gunshot range before the hunter can raise his gun.

This species, like most cockatoos, lives to a ripe old age. One bird is reported to have lived to the age of

Cockatoos

120 years. In Australia and Tasmania, their breeding season is from August to November, when two, sometimes three, eggs are laid very high up in tree hollows, and also in holes in cliffs.

Lesser Sulphur-crested Cockatoo *(Cacatua sulphurea).* Range: Celebes and Buton. This is an exact replica of the Sulphur-crested, and more suitable for the home.

Gang-gang Cockatoo *(Callocephalon fimbriatum).* Range: Victoria, New South Wales, Tasmania, King Island, and formerly in South Australia. Size 14 inches. This species is becoming rare due to the encroachment of civilization on forest lands where in the past flocks of 20 to 50 birds were common. It is still quite numerous in some sections, such as in the Otway Forest, Southern Victoria. This lovely, small species is said to have been discovered in 1803.

The body feathers are grayish, with lighter edges. The bill is horn-color, short and deep. Some of the plumage on the lower abdomen is barred with white and orange red. The cock's head is scarlet, with an erectile crest of loose, soft feathers. The shade of red in cocks varies considerably, some being bright scarlet, others a dull red. The hen's head is a lighter gray than the body, and old hens occasionally develop a few scattered red feathers on the head. The wing coverts of the hen have broader whitish edgings; flights and tail are dark gray. Immature cocks resemble hens except for the crest feathers being tipped with red, also some red feathers are on the forehead. Adult plumage is acquired at one year of age.

Gang-gangs nest in a hollow limb or tree hole high up. The breeding season is from October to January, when two white eggs are laid.

Galah *(Eolophus roseicapillus).* Range: Interior of Australia, particularly western New South Wales; occasionally found in Tasmania. Introduced in Hawaii. Size, 17½ to 18 inches. The attractive colors in this species are bluish gray on the back, shading to white. The throat, breast, and underparts are a delicate rose pink. It also has a small pink crest. Although both sexes are similar, the cock has black eyes, while the hen's are reddish brown. They make wonderful pets, as they are gentle and may be taught to say a few words. This beautiful cockatoo still exists in immense numbers in many places, being as numerous as when first officially recognized in 1817. In

Cockatoos

the wild, they feed on seeds, bulbs, and tubers.

The nest is built in hollow limbs or holes in trees and lined with green leaves. In eastern Australia, the breeding season starts in September and November; in northwestern Australia, February and March, 4 to 5 eggs being laid in a clutch.

Blue-eyed Cockatoo *(Cacatua ophthalmica)*. Range: New Britain and New Ireland. This is one of the smaller species, and is all white with crest feathers rounded instead of pointed at the tips. The bare skin around the eyes is blue. It makes a docile and intelligent pet.

Ducorps's Cockatoo *(Cacatua ducorpsii)*. Range: Solomon Islands. This species is all white with a pinkish hue over the feathers. The undersides of the wings and tail are partly yellow. The bill is horn color, and the feet are black. The sexes may be told apart by the cock having a red iris, while the hen's is brown.

Long-billed Corella *(Cacatua tenuirostris)*. Range: Inland parts of South, Western, and northwestern Australia, where it is found in pairs or flocks. Size, 18 inches. This bird has a somewhat longer upper mandible than other species described. A blue cheek patch is under the dark eyes, with a red line above the eye and round the beak. The body is white with a pink suffusion on head, breast, and chin. In the wild, this species subsists mainly on seeds, roots, bulbs, and tubers. It is said to be the best talker among cockatoos. Wild-caught birds become very docile and friendly. Hollow limbs and holes in trees are used as nests. Two to four white eggs are laid in the breeding season from August to November.

A smaller cousin is the **Little Corella** *(Cacatua sanguinea)*. Range: Inland parts of northern, central, northwestern, and South Australia and New South Wales. Three white eggs are laid in the breeding season from August to October.

Palm Cockatoo *(Probosciger aterrimus)*. Range: Papuan Islands and northern Australia. The largest specimens come from New Guinea, with those from the Aru Islands being much smaller. The largest may be up to 31 inches long, 10 of which are taken up by the tail. This is the largest of the cockatoos, and possibly the biggest psittacine bird in the world.

The body plumage is slaty black with a grayish tint, the forehead and lores being deep velvety black. Wing and tail feathers have green reflections. The large naked cheeks

Cockatiels

are pale red bordered with pale yellow. At times of excitement, the cheek skin becomes a deep blood red, as if blushing. Feet black. The bill is black and huge, with the upper mandible very long and curved. The black crest feathers are long and narrow-looking, and like an Indian headdress when elevated.

In the wild they are seen in twos and threes, and fly slowly and noiselessly. They eat various fruits and seeds, particularly the kanari nut growing on lofty forest trees (*Canarium commune*) in its habitat. This is its special food in the wild. This bird's powerful bill is specially adapted in handling this stone-hard nut which would require a blow from a heavy hammer to crack. This bird is more for a private bird collection or a zoo.

Another name for this bird of the cockatoo family is Quarrion. It is the only one of its genus, and aviculturists say that it is the connecting link between parrots and cockatoos. It was first discovered in 1788. Range: Throughout Australia. Size, 12½ to 13 inches. Scientific name: *Nymphicus hollandicus.* They are fairly safe to keep with smaller birds, unless kept with them in too small a cage.

Tamed and hand-raised Cockatiels have been taught to talk, although not comparably to the larger talking birds. Being small birds, their voice is high-pitched and hard to understand. They have a natural musical whistle. If you want to train them to talk, start when they are just out of the nest.

Description: These are gray birds with a yellow face and crest. A large white patch is on each wing. The ear coverts are orange. To tell the sexes apart, the underside coloration of the hen's tail feathers remains barred throughout life. In the mature cock, the top of the head, face, throat, and cheeks are yellow, and the crest feathers a lighter yellow at the base. The face and throat of the hen remains gray, while the orange ear coverts are duller than the cock's. Her crest is also shorter and white wing patch smaller. Both sexes may elevate or lower the crest at will.

Feeding

The staple diet for Cockatiels consists of a mixture of canary seed, large millet, hulled oats, and sunflower seed. These birds require greens, especially when feeding young. Lettuce, chickweed, dandelion, etc. may be fed. If you are in the country and don't have a grass or clover patch growing in the aviary, give them a piece of turf often. If your birds are in the city, they can do without it. A piece of cuttlebone, fresh water, bird sand, and—when molting or nesting— ground oystershell should be in their enclosure at all times. You could also hang up a millet spray, and they like a drink of milk. Vitamin-mineral supplements, as previously mentioned for other birds, may be supplied on a half slice of whole-wheat bread soaked in milk, especially when rearing young.

Breeding

An enclosure 12 to 15 feet long by 6 feet high by 6 feet wide should be used. Five feet of this should consist of a shelter with a solid roof and sides, the rest an open flight.

In the wild, the Cockatiel nests in hollow limbs of dead trees. Use plywood for making an oblong nest box 16 inches long by 8 inches high by 6 inches wide. A 1½-inch thick block of wood should be scooped out, making a concave hollow ¾ inch deep and 6 inches wide, to prevent the eggs rolling around and getting chilled. Put insecticide powder on the nest bottom, then place this block over it, with the concave section toward the rear. If the back of the nest box is screwed or nailed to this block, it may be pulled out like a drawer for cleaning and inspection. A thin layer of sawdust or peatmoss may be placed in the hollow to cradle the eggs and absorb droppings. A 6-inch landing perch should be placed just below the 3-inch-diameter entrance hole, which should be near the top. The nest box may be attached to the roof or to an upright post. Another type of nest box would be a log split or sawed in half, hollowed out to large-enough dimensions, with a 3-inch entrance hole at top, landing perch, and bottom made concave with a gouge. This could be hinged together in the rear, and a hook-and-eye would fasten the front.

Budgerigars

Both adult birds of a pair should be over one year old to breed. Cocks are suitable for breeding from 6 to 8 years, the hens less than that. One pair only should be in an enclosure if being bred. When not breeding, more may be kept together in an aviary. They lay from 5 to 8 eggs, which are laid and hatched in rotation, requiring 20 days incubation. The cock relieves the hen by day during the incubation. The parents are good feeders and usually rear the whole brood. The young are strange-looking, with silky yellow down. They hiss and rock sideways when being fed. Two or three broods at the most should be permitted, to maintain the vigor of the parents. Young cocks may be distinguished from the hens when a few weeks old by their having more yellow on the face or, if even younger, by having a paler face before the yellow feathers appear. The nestlings have shorter crests than the adults, although the cocks' crests are better developed; young cocks are also noisier than hens.

Scientific name: *Melopsittacus undulatus*. Range: Australia. Size of a Canary. This parakeet is included in this book not so much for its talking inclinations which may be slight, but for the truly astounding color range which skillful breeders and the species's peculiar genetic makeup have produced to delight the fancier's eye. The present color varieties number more than 100, with new mutations developing constantly. Black and red shades have not been included as yet, although mutations in these colors have been reported in such distant places as New Zealand and South Africa. Budgerigars have quaint mannerisms which are attractive also, making them desirable exotic-looking pets.

Budgerigars were discovered early in the nineteenth century. The first specimen to reach England was shot in 1804. During the year 1840, the great naturalist John Gould brought the first pairs of wild-caught light green Budgies to England, where they soon became popular cage birds there and in Europe.

It is estimated that today Budgerigars exist in greater numbers in Australia than in Gould's day. For many years it has not paid trappers to catch them for

Budgerigars

the pet market, as millions of superior birds in all colors have been bred in captivity, where they are almost as numerous in aviculturists' hands as they are in the wild. Budgerigars are found generally throughout central Australia, and in the southern parts are migratory, appearing in huge flocks in spring when grass seeds are plentiful, and migrating northwards when their breeding season is over. Breeding color varieties has been carried on mainly in England, where these birds exceed the Canary in general popularity. The name given to these parakeets by the natives of Australia was "Budgerigar," by which they are commonly referred to today. Budgerigars are happiest when kept in pairs or even in colonies (when not breeding). Fanciers, who breed for color, separate the sexes entirely during the nonbreeding season. Contrary to popular opinion, if one of a pair dies, the one left will not pine away; another mate will be acceptable, as cocks especially are notoriously unfaithful.

Talking and Tricks

Budgies, like other smaller talking birds, have small voices hard to understand, and do not compare with the more proficient talkers dealt with in this manual. They may be taught to talk by following the suggestions given in the chapters on taming and talking.

The cock makes a better talker than the hen. During the months you are training him (from 2 to 8 months old), it is advisable to keep him away from others of his kind unless you have a good tutor. He should already be hand-tamed. No bird can be taught to talk if it is wild and nervous.

Budgerigars, and others such as lories, may be taught many tricks. Tiny bird playgrounds consisting of swings, trapeze, etc. may be ordered from your pet store for these birds. You and your bird will both enjoy one.

If you keep two or more Budgies in small cages, they would benefit by some wing exercise if you should let them fly around the room for 20 minutes once or twice a day. You will find that these birds all fly together in circles around the room, coming to rest at the highest perching spot. You may follow them around with a small stick, much as the pigeon fancier exercises his birds. When tired, they will fly right back to their cage. During the breeding season, this method of

Budgerigars

exercising should not be attempted. Of course, windows and doors must be closed before letting them out.

Feeding

A mixture of the following seeds which you can make up yourself by purchasing them separately, or buy mixed in package form, makes up their staple diet. White millet, hulled oats, canary seed—the mixture is two parts millet to one part canary and one part oats.

A mixture of other bird seeds may be given for variety. If available, your Budgies will appreciate a sprig of spray millet. If you are out in the country, or I will cut it for them, fresh seeding heads of grasses and grains will be much relished; besides which, seeds in the fresh stage supply vitamins and minerals which are lacking or are diminished in dry seed. In the wild, grass seeds form the diet of these parakeets.

Fresh greens and a piece of apple or pear should be supplied daily also. Cod-liver oil, given in cold weather, may be added to their diet by letting several drops soak into their seed overnight, or a teaspoonful of oil to a pint of seed (mix well.) The powdered vitamin-mineral supplements mentioned in the diet of every other bird in the book may be given to Budgies by placing a pinch on a piece of whole-wheat bread dipped in milk, or given alone in a side dish. It will never harm them if given alone, and the birds won't take too much of it.

Other daily requirements are: Fresh water in a clean font, bird sand in a side dish, and for their calcium needs, either fasten a cuttlebone near a perch or place a small dish of ground oyster shell in their cage. This is important, especially during breeding or molting.

Bathing

Budgerigars, like most psittacines, don't bathe in a pan as other birds do. They prefer to roll in wet grass if you have a patch of it in an outdoor enclosure. If you keep them in a small cage, place enough wet cabbage, lettuce, or other vegetable leaves near their perch for them to wet themselves with, as well as to eat. Spraying them with water from a mister, especially if you exhibit them in bird shows, will start them preening. Parrots also enjoy being out in a gentle summer rain. The English bird newspaper *Cage and Aviary Birds* gives an excellent

Budgerigars

suggestion for encouraging Budgies to bathe when kept in an outdoor aviary. This is done by piercing two small holes in a tin can, one inch from the edges. This is filled with water and placed on the wire mesh forming the roof of the flight. Directly underneath, attached to the flight-cage roof beneath the center of the can, hang lettuce or cabbage leaves or long tufts of grass, allowing the water to drip slowly on the greens. Immediately below, where the greens will touch it, place a perch. Budgies will greatly enjoy rolling in the wet greens, especially in summer.

Breeding

Breeding pairs of Budgerigars should be one year old. The hens begin laying in March in the United States, and no more than three clutches a season should be permitted each pair. If you have more nests than that, the parents will be debilitated for another breeding season, and the young won't have the stamina and size of earlier hatches. Cocks and hens should be placed in separate flights after the third brood. You can tell that a pair is in breeding condition when the cock's cere is bright blue, and he is very active and attentive towards the hen—that is, more than usual. A hen in high breeding condition will have the cere dark brown and corrugated.

About five eggs form the average clutch, although some pairs produce from eight to ten. If one pair has more eggs than can be properly covered by the hen's body, they may be transferred among other sitting hens. Eggs are laid on alternate days, and incubation lasts 17-18 days, the young hatching in sequence. They are fed with regurgitated food from the parent's crop. Young birds only a few weeks old are very difficult to sex. The quickest way to pick out the cocks is to look at the cere (a fleshy patch above the bill in which the nostrils are placed). In the young cocks, the cere is more rounded and stands out more than in the young hens, whose cere is flatter. When young, both sexes will have very pale ceres, but the cock's cere is a little deeper blue, particularly near the nostrils. The immature hen's cere may be light tan or pale blue. When the young are up to six weeks old, they have fine black stripes across the forehead, which disappear afterwards. This is the time to select the young cocks to train as talkers.

In Australia, Budgerigars live in

Budgerigars

large flocks, feeding on grass seeds and nesting in tall eucalyptus trees.

The Breeding Cage

If you don't have much room and wish to breed Budgerigars in the house or apartment, you can make or buy your own breeding cage. If you build your own, the dimensions should be 24 inches long by 24 inches high by 18 inches wide. Except for the perches, it is not necessary to use any other wood whatsoever in its construction. To make a real neat, manufactured-looking breeding cage, half- or three-quarter-inch galvanized wire mesh should be used for the sides and roof. Aluminum molding strips are used for framing the sides, top, and base; it can be either three-fourths inch or one inch.

Aluminum molding is better for cage framing than wood, easy to drill holes in or to cut with a small utility saw. It is obtainable in the bigger hardware or linoleum stores, where a good selection of many types and sizes are available. Small brass or aluminum bolts, nuts, and lock washers should be used in fastening framing and base. Small brass or aluminum corner angles may be used in connecting the side

molding strips to the base and roof. The small lock washers may only be available in iron, in which case dip them in a little spar varnish to prevent rust.

The sections of wire mesh will fit into the inside grooves. Wire mesh may be cut to proper size for top and sides with a metal shears. To install the wire mesh for the roof, slide it along the inside horizontal grooves of the molding, leaving one end open. When in place, bolt the remaining molding section in place, fitting the edge of the mesh into its groove beforehand.

Front view and cross-section of a strip of aluminum molding—the inside grooves hold the wire-mesh section in place.

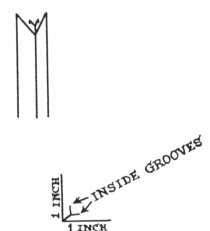

Budgerigars

For the floor, you can make a one-inch-deep tray out of sheet metal, which can be either galvanized, or copper or aluminum. Galvanized is the cheapest. The sides of the sheet metal should be bent over one inch all around, the corners cut and neatly soldered together. A small glass knob or plastic handle, such as is used for cupboard doors, may be fastened to the front side of the tray in the center to enable you to pull it out of the cage for cleaning.

To form the base, four angle sections of aluminum are required, cut to proper size and bolted together with small metal angles on the inside at each corner. For the front end, out of which the metal tray will slide, fasten a 24-inch-long angle section just above the one-inch-high tray. The wire mesh forming the front wall may be slid down the inside grooves of the corner frames and will be stopped by resting on the section you just put in. Thus nothing will interfere with the easy sliding in and out of the tray.

The above specifications cover the construction of the smallest breeding cage for one pair of Budgies only. If you have ground to spare in the rear of your home, it is much better to build breeding enclosures such as have been described earlier in this book. For Budgies, the dimensions need be only 12 feet long by 5 feet wide by 6 feet high. No more than 3 pairs of Budgies should be kept in each section to prevent the hens fighting over nest boxes or killing one another's young. Each enclosure should contain only birds of one color variety, to control your breeding expectations. Keeping only three pairs in a flight also produces more young than using a colony system of indiscriminate breeding.

Nest Boxes

The rectangular nest box is suitable for Budgerigars, lovebirds, lories, hanging-parrots, pygmy-parrots, Cockatiels, caiques, conures, parrotlets, and the larger parakeets, so long as its size is appropriate.

Various styles of nest boxes may be made. The coconut husk used to be popular among fanciers but has been discarded because of the ease in which mites bred among the fibres. The approximate size of a nest box for Budgies should be 9 inches high by 6 inches wide and deep. Plywood makes a satisfactory material for nest boxes. The roof should be slanted down from back to front, forming an overhang to prevent other hens or cocks roosting

Budgerigars

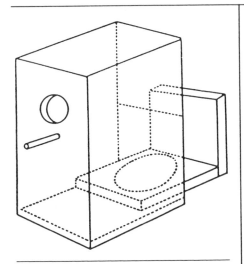

Nest box in which the concave block is attached to the rear wall—this arrangement facilitates cleaning and inspection.

on it. The entrance hole should be 1½ inches in diameter, barely large enough for the hen to crawl through. Large nesting holes have been known to deter breeding, as hens like to feel secure when sitting. The bottom of the nest box should have a removable 1½-inch-thick block of wood, made concave by scooping out a hollow ¾-inch deep at the center, and 4½ inches across. The concave block is necessary to prevent the eggs from rolling to a corner of the nest and becoming chilled. Some insecticide powder may be applied under the block for mites. The rear wall of the nest box should be screwed to the wood

block. Both parts will be removable from the rest of the box, making cleaning and inspection easier.

Budgerigars don't build nests, so you may add some peat moss or damp turf in the bottom. Install a perch on the outside near the entrance hole. This can be a dowel ½ inch in diameter and six inches long. To enable the parent birds to clamber in and out easily, a good suggestion is to fasten a small strip of ½-inch wire mesh inside the box from the floor to the entrance hole. To prevent fighting among the hens for nesting sites, all nest boxes in an enclosure should be the same in construction and all placed at the same height. By hanging the boxes where the entrance hole faces the light, the hens will be able to see better while feeding the young. Also supply a couple more nest boxes than there are pairs in the enclosure to prevent fighting. These nest-box arrangements are used by successful breeders who have found out by observation how to produce more and healthier young from Budgerigars.

The Larger Parakeets

Among the most beautiful and varied species of psittacine birds must be mentioned the larger parakeets, which constitute a large group. They exist in most tropical places in the world. Though many are highly colored, few if any will talk. The English bird fanciers have really done wonders in propagating these lovely birds, particularly since for several years they weren't permitted to import fresh wild stock due to the psittacosis scare. Species which are nearing extinction in their native Australia because of the encroachment of civilization in their habitats have been successfully bred in England. It is possible to acclimate many of these larger parakeets so that they will thrive in outdoor aviaries in temperate climates the year round.

When shipping the larger parakeets, it is better to pack each individual in a separate crate or carton. If a few are sent in one crate to save shipping space and costs, put individual birds in separate cartons or make compartments in the one crate. This advice is given because the larger parakeets are given to having fatal fights if kept close together on a trip. This applies even to pairs mated a long time.

Feeding

These birds require a staple seed diet of sunflower seed, canary seed, large red or yellow millet, hulled oats, buckwheat in hull or as groats, and also wheat, which is a very hard seed and is best given soaked overnight. You may purchase these separately and mix them yourself, or purchase them ready-mixed in a package.

Large parakeets should be given greens daily. If you scatter some seed on a patch of damp peatmoss in a sunny spot, they will sprout and supply young, green growth. An apple or pear should be stuck on a perch holder. Cod-liver oil may be supplied by placing a few drops on this fruit, making a cut in it first to retain the oil. The birds will start eating the fruit where you made the cut. Give the previously mentioned food supplements, a pinch on milk-soaked whole-wheat bread, or mixed in with grated raw carrot, hard-boiled egg, or mashed potatoes. A length of spray millet should be hung up in the cage often.

Breeding

In breeding, the larger parakeets require an outdoor flight with

The Larger Parakeets

attached shelter about 15 feet long by 6 feet high by 6 feet wide, the construction of which should be the same as that explained earlier. Parakeets, especially those of the Australian broad-tail group, are fighters among themselves and only one pair should be bred in an enclosure. If you are breeding them in flights side by side in a row, have double wiring, leaving a six-inch space between the flights for cleaning out leaves and rubbish. This is suggested, otherwise the cocks will have vicious fights through the wires, and your breeding operations will be nil.

The larger parakeets make good parents, but the young should be removed from them as soon as they are feeding themselves or the adults show signs of wanting to nest again. All this advice will help to forestall some of the difficulties in raising these beautiful birds. There will be other problems to handle as they come up, depending on each pair or species. This makes for the fascination of the hobby to the fancier.

Eastern Rosella *(Platycercus eximius)*. Top of head, face, breast, and under tail coverts scarlet. Chin and throat white. Hindneck, scapulars, and inner wing coverts velvety black, broadly edged with brighter green. Back, rump, and upper tail coverts grass green. Central tail feathers dark green; outer ones, pale lilac. Outer wing coverts lilac. Primary flight feathers black and blue. Bill yellowish. Legs and feet blue gray. The hen is similar with less scarlet. You are sure it is a hen if a small spot of green is on the nape.

Northern Rosella *(Platycercus venustus)*. Northern Australia. This species is said to be the most beautiful. The breast and rump are pale yellow, each feather having a dark edging at the tip, producing a scaly effect. The head is velvety black. Cheek patches white with dark blue on lower edge. The feathers of the mantle are black with cream edgings. Wings are violet with longitudinal black patches near the shoulder. Central tail feathers are violet, outer ones blue. Under tail coverts red. Bill light blue gray. The hen is similar but has a smaller head and bill and duller coloring.

Other Rosellas are: Pale-headed Rosella *(Platycercus adscitus)*; Western Rosella *(Platycercus icterotis)*; Crimson Rosella *(Platycercus elegans)*; Adelaide Rosella *(Platycercus adelaidae)*; Yellow Rosella *(Platycercus flaveolus)*; Green Rosella *(Platycercus caledonicus)*.

The Larger Parakeets

As parakeets go, rosellas are not noisy, but have a musical whistle. They are best kept in an aviary rather than in a cage. They lay four to six eggs in a clutch. When acclimated, they are hardy enough to be left out all year round in an unheated aviary. The sexes are alike. To tell them apart the quickest way, the hens have small greenish brown feathers at the back of the eyes which cocks don't have. Nest boxes for these larger parakeets should be oblong, 16 inches long by 10 inches high by 8 inches wide. Have a concave block of wood inside as is described for Budgerigars.

Another one of the many attractive large Australian Parakeets is the **Princess Parakeet** *(Polytelis alexandrae)*. Central and western Australia. This is a slim bird in beautiful pastel shades. Cock: Mantle, olive, and crown, light blue; wing coverts, yellowish green; rump, violet (just the males have this). The throat and thighs are pink, breast and abdomen gray green, under tail coverts olive. Central tail feathers olive and very long. The outer tail feathers have the inner webs rose. The bill is coral red. Hen: Tail is shorter, rump slate color, crown grayish mauve, wing coverts darker green. Bill dark red. The young resemble the hen and acquire adult plumage when between 12 and 15 months old. Young cocks have larger, flatter heads and are brighter in the crown.

Asiatic Parakeets

Typical of the Asiatic parakeets is the **Alexandrine Parakeet** *(Psitt.. la eupatria nepalensis)*. This beautiful, sleek-feathered parakeet has been kept in cages since ancient times, and becomes very affectionate and attached to its owner. They are widely kept in India as a favorite cage bird. This is one of the largest, if not the largest, parakeet, and is not as common as its close relative, the Rose-ringed Parakeet *(Psittacula krameri)*. There are four other races

Photographs on pages 57-64: 57—Sun Conure pair (Aratinga solstitialis). 58—Brown-throated Conure (Aratinga pertinax aeruginosa). 59—Red-lored Amazon (Amazona autumnalis). 60—Lories feeding (Trichoglossus and Eos spp.). 62—Edwards's Fig-Parrot (Psittaculirostris edwardsii). 63—Red-rumped Parrot pair (Psephotus haematonotus). 64—Superb Parrot pair (Polytelis swainsonii).

The Larger Parakeets

of the Alexandrine, having minor differences in size and coloration, which are found in India excepting the northwestern desert area.

Alexandrines are large parakeets about 20 inches long, with grass-green plumage, darker green on wings, which have a maroon patch on the shoulders. The head is large for the body in all races, having a short, massive, deeply hooked upper mandible. A black edging runs from under the lower mandible around the cheeks. The rose collar around the sides and back of the neck in cocks is absent in the hens, which makes them easy to sex. The tail is very long, almost a foot, and pointed.

The staple food for Alexandrines is a mixture of sunflower, hulled oats, large millet, raw peanuts, and canary seed. Other seeds may be added for variety, such as wheat, cracked corn (dry or soaked overnight in water), buckwheat, and hemp. A few almonds and walnuts will be relished if given occasionally.

A portion of cut-up fruits, grapes, and berries is beneficial. Other suitable items, if you have them available, are: fresh corn on cob, fresh peas in the pod, dry whole-wheat bread, dog biscuit, dates, figs, grated hard-boiled egg yolk, corn or brown rice boiled in milk, celery stalk, raw carrot, fresh beet tops, lettuce, cabbage, sprays of fresh oats.

Breeding

Alexandrines are free breeders when suitably mated and given proper accommodations. In the wild, many pairs may breed in a colony; however, in captivity it is preferable to have only one pair in a flight.

A breeding pair requires an outdoor flight about 18 feet long by 6 feet wide by 6 feet high, having an enclosed 4-foot-long shelter as a retreat from rain, wind, or sun. A Cockatiel nest box 16 inches long by 8 inches high by 6 inches wide, made of plywood, with a 3-inch-diameter hole near the top makes an appropriate nest box. The floor should have a 1½-inch-thick block of wood, gouged out to make a ¾-inch-deep concave hollow, which prevents the eggs from rolling to the sides and getting chilled. A little sawdust may be placed in the hollow to steady the eggs. Some successful breeders use a small piece of fresh turf, roots up, as a nest bottom, as the dampness aids in hatching. The nest box should be placed high in the flight.

The Larger Parakeets

A small nail keg with the top boarded up except for a small hole is fine also, and doesn't require a concave block, as it should be hung on its side high up in the flight. These parakeets do not require any nesting material.

The breeding season is from December to April. The eggs are all white, oval, and blunted at both ends, numbering 2 to 5 in a clutch. Incubation requires 21 days, and both parents incubate in turns and feed the young. When two months of age, the young are fully feathered and come out of the nest. They attain adult plumage after their second molt, the immature birds being a duller green coloring than the hen. Young Alexandrines are very desirable, as they will learn to speak a few words which, combined with their affectionate nature and wanting attention, makes them quite appealing.

In the wild, Alexandrines prefer woodland near cultivated grain fields and orchards, which they plunder freely. They also have a liking for berries and tropical flowers. Like the crows and Common Mynahs I've noticed in India, Alexandrines fly in the evening to community roosts; wave after wave wing their way to the preferred groves and bicker for the choicest branches, till the setting sun puts an end to their chatter. With the rising morning sun there is an exodus to their feeding grounds.

Alexandrines can be kept in a large parrot cage, where they may be permitted to go in and out at times when you are with them. Windows and doors should be closed then, of course.

Another desirable Asiatic parakeet which is much smaller (9 inches) is *Psittacula cyanocephala*, the **Plum-headed Parakeet**. There are three races: South India and Ceylon (*P. c. cyanocephala*), North India and Assam (*P. c. bengalensis*), and Burma (*P. c. roseata*). This is a pretty, docile, small parakeet, very common as a pet in India. In Calcutta and Bombay, native boys have followed me in the street with these birds on their fingers. Perhaps they were either tamed, doped, or had their flight feathers cut. At any rate, I was very tempted to purchase them but, being in the army, was unable to keep them. Their body is green with maroon shoulder patches. The most attractive part—the head—is a lovely shade of bluish red. The hen lacks shoulder patches and the head is blue gray.

Lories

These birds are found only in the Australian region and among the many South Seas islands.

Lories and lorikeets are differentiated by the former having a short, broad tail, while the latter have long pointed ones. Lorikeets are smaller than lories. They both possess the most brilliant colors of all the psittacine birds, and are the only ones which have brush-tipped tongues instead of the smooth tip of the other psittacines. Lorikeets are about 6 to 8 inches long, and lories from 7 to 12 inches.

These birds are recommended for the experienced fancier only. They are rather expensive, and, although not difficult to keep, a fancier who has kept birds already will better understand their wants. The amusement they will give you is well worth the expense. Lorikeets especially are real bird comedians, constantly active, clambering around the cage wire, twisting around their perches, swinging from a branch upside down, and doing other acrobatics. Their voices are squeaky and shrill, and they are swift fliers, so be careful when entering their aviary. These birds do not talk, except perhaps for the Chattering Lory, which may say a few words. Lories seem to display more intelligence than other psittacine birds. They are dificult to sex, but the cock is usually a little brighter in coloring.

General Care

Lories have very liquid droppings, hence if kept in a two-foot-square cage, the newspaper with sand, peatmoss, or sawdust should be changed every evening. These birds don't thrive so well in a cage, however, and if you can give them a larger enclosure, it would suit them better. They enjoy frequent bathing every sunny morning, and should be given a large-enough flower-pot saucer in which to do this. This unglazed pottery is very satisfactory for small birds, as they won't slip around too much when splashing.

Feeding

In the wild, these birds live on blossoms and flower nectar (which their brushy tongue enables them to secure), soft fruits like bananas, paw-paws, mangos, and berries. Never feed lories or lorikeets on seeds even if they will eat them. Many fanciers have found out, to their chagrin, that sooner or later a seed diet will bring on paralysis of the legs, or fits which will prove fatal. Sunflower is a soft seed, and a very few grains may be given to them as part of their regular diet. Their systems cannot properly handle hard seeds.

In captivity a varied diet may be given them. This may consist of brown or wild rice boiled in milk with brown sugar or honey added, boiled corn, or a piece of fresh corn on the cob. Fruits are good when fed with something more solid like mashed potatoes or yams. Soaked raisins, grapes, cherries, berries, fresh fruits in season, canned fruit salad, and canned baby foods are good. Soaked in milk or in honey thinned with water, you may give fruit cake, sponge cake, or whole-wheat bread (which, incidentally, may be buttered) and also dried dates or figs soaked in hot water. Fresh greens should be supplied daily, such as dandelion, chickweed, lettuce, green celery stalk, sprouted seed, etc. If you have a garden and can give them some fresh flowers such as morning glory, four-o'clocks, etc., they will extract the nectar from them. It is particularly advisable in feeding these birds that a small daily pinch of a vitamin-mineral supplement be added on their food. In winter give a few drops of cod-liver oil, and

hang up a strip of bacon. During breeding or molting, a pinch of fish or bone meal should be added daily. Fresh water should always be before them. Some fanciers make their own nectar of honey or maple syrup thinned with water, and placed in a small side dish. If you want to really tame them, offer a tablespoon full of milk. They will hold the spoon with a foot while drinking. The large variety of nutritional items are given because most fanciers don't know what to feed these birds, and many haven't even heard of them.

Breeding

Lories aren't too difficult to breed if the proper accommodations are supplied them. An enclosure 8 feet long by 5 feet wide by 6 feet high will do for up to three pairs. One pair to a flight is better. Fresh tree branches should be placed at either end. In keeping any bird in an aviary, it is better not to place any perches in the center; thus more space will be available for flight from one end to the other.

For a nest, a hollow log or plywood nest box such as is used for Budgerigars will be suitable. In the concave nest block, place a thin layer of either damp peatmoss,

Lories

sawdust, or turf with roots up. These birds like nest boxes to sleep in also. Two to five eggs will be laid in a clutch, depending on the species. The young are reared with regurgitated food. If you should have to feed the young by hand, use a medicine dropper. In hand-feeding you may vary a nestling's diet with honey thinned with water, plain milk, or canned baby foods thinned out with milk or water. When hand-raising nestlings, a small pinch of a mineral concentrate may be mixed in the formula. When they become older, oatmeal or Pablum moistened with water may be fed with a toothpick.

A few species of lories are mentioned here:

Rainbow Lory *(Trichoglossus haematodus)*. Range: New Guinea to Celebes, and in eastern Australia from Cape York to Victoria, also Tasmania. This may be one of the prettiest of the lories. The head and throat are a brilliant purplish blue. Nape of neck greenish yellow, abdomen blue. Under tail coverts yellow at the base and green at tip. Under wing coverts are red with mottled red breast. Feet slate gray, bill red with yellow tip. Truly a rainbow-colored bird. Length 12 inches, of which 5½ inches is tail. Sexes very similar, with the hen a little paler.

In the wild, they associate in small flocks, but do migrate periodically in Australia, flying at great heights in huge flocks when blossoms of honeysuckle and gum trees are open. The hen lays 3 to 4 eggs. They often have been bred in captivity. The young in first plumage have the breast yellow with hardly any tinge of red; also the greenish yellow band of the adult is scarcely visible. The Rainbow Lory is mainly an aviary bird. A subspecies, *Trichoglossus h. rubritorquis,* from northern Australia, has a bright orange breast and a red collar.

Papuan Lory *(Charmosyna papou stellae)*. Range: Southeast New Guinea. This is said to be the loveliest of all. The body is bright red, with a black patch on the neck tipped with blue. Wings and upper back are green, abdomen dark blue. The tail feathers are long, delicate filaments of green, red, orange, and yellow. The sexes may be told apart, as the rump in the cock is scarlet and blue, while in the hen it is yellow and blue. This species is difficult to obtain, and is extremely rare in collections.

Yellow-streaked Lory *(Chalcopsitta sintillata chloroptera)*. Range: New Guinea.

Lories

Chattering Lory *(Lorius garrulus flavopalliatus)*. Range: Moluccas. This subspecies is a shining scarlet with a beautiful golden yellow patch on its back.

Blue-crowned Lory *(Vini australis)*. Range: Samoa and the Fiji Islands. Body green, with cheeks, throat, and middle abdomen red. The crown is blue, lower abdomen dark purple. Bill and feet are orange red. This very common bird lives in flocks.

Purple-naped Lory *(Lorius domicellus)*. Range: Ceram and Amboina. Its length is twelve inches, and it is one of the most beautifully colored birds known. Most of the body feathers are scarlet, which do not fade in captivity like many other red-feathered birds. The breast has a gold band. Wings are green with blue on the edges and under wing coverts. The tail is red, having a band at the tip which is dark purple red above, and golden red below. The cap on the head is deep purplish black.

The brush on the tongue of this species is less developed than in other lories, and is less dependent on a liquid diet. They are usually found in small parties of six or so, where they may be seen eating the soft fruits of the various kinds of wild figs. Purple-napes usually lay 3 to 4 eggs on the bare wood in some hollow branch, although a nest box as described for the larger parakeets would be more appropriate in captivity.

This bird makes just about the perfect bird pet, being most remarkable for its gentle and affectionate disposition. It also can be taught to talk. This, together with its gorgeous plumage, makes it much in demand as a pet. They become very attached to their owners. They will do a dance and bang their bills on the surface where they are resting in accompaniment to their owner hitting his knuckles on a table in front of them. They are remarkable ventriloquists, throwing their voices to the opposite side of a room.

Black-capped Lory *(Lorius lory)*. Range: New Guinea. This is a close relative of the Purple-nape, although it does not have a yellow band, and the entire abdomen is blue, with throat red, wings green, and black cap. It also makes an affectionate, colorful pet.

Unusual Parrots

Hanging-parrots are tiny birds (5 inches), mostly bright green with a short, round tail, and having a shrill whistle and undulating flight. They are birds of the woods. While they don't have the brush-tipped tongue of the lories, the method of feeding is exactly the same, as they are nectar and soft-fruit eaters also. These species, too, are for the experienced aviculturist only, as they are delicate in captivity. They may bathe on sunny mornings.

Hanging-parrots make amusing pets, and have the habit of sleeping or just resting upside down (like a bat) from a perch, which should be a tree branch renewed occasionally. A locking joint in the foot enables them to do this. In the house, a two-foot-square cage will accommodate them. Outdoors in summer, a six-foot enclosure will do, especially if you wish to breed them. A hollow log or one of the Budgerigar nest boxes with a concave block is suitable for them. They lay three small, white, round eggs, and their natural breeding season is between January and April. It is best, to prevent egg binding in the hen, to delay their breeding till March in the United States.

In Calcutta, I saw a cage full of these small birds, which were sold reasonably. I couldn't believe my eyes, and had to get closer to see them all hanging upside down from the top of the wooden-barred cage. At my approach, they became frightened and dropped down so hard that I thought they had cracked their skulls. The Indian natives keep them as pets, as they do in Malaya and the Philippines. Among the various species are:

Vernal Hanging-Parrot (*Loriculus vernalis*). India, Burma, and the Andaman Islands. Body bright green with crimson rump. The cock has a small blue throat-patch which is absent in the hen.

Yellow-throated Hanging-Parrot (*Loriculus pusillus*). Java and Bali. Bill light red, green body, brighter on the head. Yellow on mantle and throat. Lower back and upper tail coverts scarlet, blue under the wings and tail. The hen is similar, but without the yellow throat.

Blue-crowned Hanging-Parrot (*Loriculus galgulus*). Malaya, Sumatra, Borneo. This is a common bird of the forest that occasionally enters native gardens, feeding mostly on fruit. Body green, with red breast and rump, yellow patches on mantle and lower back. Bill is black. The cock has a blue crown

Unusual Parrots

patch absent in the hen. She has duller colors, with a yellowish breast and suffusion on the mantle.

Ceylon Hanging-Parrot (*Loriculus beryllinus*). Ceylon. Body bright green and back red. The cock has a red crown patch absent in the hen.

Philippine Hanging-Parrot (*Loriculus philippensis*). Native name, *colasisi*. This is a very common bird often kept in cages by the Filipinos. The bill is slender, and the short square tail has some blue in it. The body is bright green, with scarlet rump and forehead. There is an orange scarlet patch on the throat and breast of the cocks. The hens have a pale blue face and throat. Immatures resemble the hens, and the nestlings are green with a red rump. There are 11 subspecies among the various Philippine Islands.

Fig-Parrots

These are among the rarer psittacine birds, so named because they feed on the fruits of tall, wild fig trees of the jungle, and also native berries, in company with fruit-pigeons and other frugivorous birds. Fig-parrots are mostly a beautiful green shade, hence difficult to see in the trees. They are very quiet, with the main indications of their presence being partly eaten figs which tumble down while they are feeding. Little is known about these birds, and in captivity they would probably require a diet of soft food with some fruit.

The **Double-eyed Fig-Parrot** is found in Australia and New Guinea. *Opopsitta diophthalma coxeni* occurs in southeastern Queensland and northeastern New South Wales. It is a short-tailed green parrot 5 inches long, with large head and massive black beak. Yellow patches on sides of breast, with red tips on inner wing feathers. In the cock, ear coverts and part of face red. Forehead and lower cheeks are blue. The hen has less red on the face and on ear coverts. They nest in a hollow stump, and lay 2 white eggs.

Opopsitta diophthalma macleayana, found in northern Queensland, has a yellow patch on its breast and red tips on inner wing feathers. Adult cock has a small red patch on forehead and on side of face. Below the red cheek patch and around the eye is blue coloring. Adult hen has the red face replaced with blue. Immatures are duller and paler than adult hen. They nest in a hole in a tree about 40 feet from the ground

Unusual Parrots

and lay 3 or 4 white eggs. They breed from September to November.

In *Opopsitta diophthalma marshalli,* from the Cape York Peninsula, the cock has a red forehead with a narrow yellow band behind it and red cheek patches with blue below them. In the hen, the forehead is blue, and cheeks buff with blue below them. Immature cocks are like the hen, but have some red on face.

Pygmy-Parrots

Since this book is to cover all psittacine birds, the pygmy-parrots, smallest psittacine birds in the world, will be mentioned. These tiny midgets are no bigger than your thumb. They are delicate in captivity, and are practically unobtainable for the average fancier. Their color is mostly green, and size ranges from 3 to 3½ inches.

Little is known of their feeding habits, except that they feed on termites and on certain fungi in their habitat. The stiffened shafts of their tail feathers help to keep the birds propped up when they are feeding on termites that live in tree colonies. Pygmy-parrots also excavate their nesting holes in termite nests. They are birds of the jungle, where, being sociable, they fly in small flocks, giving out their sibilant call notes.

Some species are found in New Guinea, and others are:

Finsch's Pygmy-Parrot *(Micropsitta finschii).* Range: Solomon Islands. Mostly green, with bill and feet gray, and the iris orange. The cock has a pink cere, the hen gray. Five subspecies exist. 3 to 3½ inches.

Red-breasted Pygmy-Parrot *(Micropsitta bruijnii).* Range: Solomon Islands. 3½ inches. The cock has the hindneck and sides of throat brilliant blue; crown, cheeks and ear coverts, pink. Back, wings and sides, green; center of abdomen and under tail coverts, rose. The hen is green above with yellowish abdomen and blue crown.

Eclectus Parrot

This parrot exhibits a remarkable coloration, which occurs only in this species. The cocks are bright green with red side markings, while the hens are red with blue side markings. For some time zoologists took them to be different species. Ten subspecies of *Eclectus roratus* occur on New Guinea and nearby islands, ranging in size from 11 to

Diseases and Health Problems

13 inches. Cock: Green body with outer wings and tail feathers blue. A red patch under the wings extends to the flanks. Upper bill and iris, orange. Feet and lower bill, black. Hen: Head and throat, bright red. Back, wings, and thighs, dark red. Underwing and a band running across upper back and abdomen, blue. Flight feathers blue. Tail, red with pale tips.

The feeding of this species is the same as that given for larger parakeets. Furnished the proper nesting arrangements, they are not difficult to breed. Only one breeding pair should be in an enclosure. The nest box made of plywood boards or from a hollowed-out log should be about 18 to 20 inches high by 12 inches wide by 12 inches deep. A hollowed-out wooden block should be on the bottom for the eggs. The entrance hole near the top should be 4 inches in diameter, with an 8-inch landing perch fastened on the outside.

The best way of controlling disease is by keeping your bird cages and bird premises clean at all times, free of dampness, out of strong winds or drafts, and where the sun can reach in part of the day. A proper diet combining all essential vitamins and minerals maintains vitality, hardiness, and longevity. Food dishes and especially water receptacles should have any sliminess or dirt scoured out daily with hot water and washing soda. For soft-food or nectar feeders, make a fresh supply every day, and don't place the food dish in the sun where it will sour or dry out.

Newly purchased birds added to your collection should be quarantined for 3 to 4 weeks before introducing them into your stock.

Since many of the different illnesses that befall birds have similar signs, an examination by an experienced avian veterinarian offers the best hope of a correct diagnosis and successful treatment. Usually, laboratory tests are needed.

A Hospital Cage

If your bird is ill in any way, before giving it any other remedy, the best treatment for it is heat at

Diseases and Health Problems

85 to 90 F., maintained during the day and especially at night, till your bird is bright-eyed and active again. To accomplish this, you will have to make or buy a hospital cage. This can be nothing more than a wooden box large enough for the bird, and lined on the inside with ½-inch insulation board all around. A six-foot electric cord is required, together with an electric light bulb installed at one end of the box. At the opposite end, put in a thermometer that will be visible from the outside through a glass window installed in the wall next to it. This window will permit observation of the bird also.

The only ventilation will come through half-inch holes (about 8), which you will drill in the top of the box at the opposite end, away from the light connection. The electric bulb should supply the required heat to maintain 85 to 90 F. inside the box when the room temperature outside is 60 to 65 F. It is better to put in a stronger light bulb than necessary rather than a weaker one. This treatment is worthless if less than 85 F. is maintained. If the temperature in the hospital cage goes up too much above 90 F., it may be controlled if you include a dimmer. This permits you to decrease the temperature by

reducing the voltage to the bulb, or to increase it.

The bright glare of the bulb can be eliminated by placing it toward the bottom of the box (heat rises) and attaching a piece of sheet metal two inches away from the bulb. It is advisable also to place a section of ½-inch wire mesh around the bulb if the bird you put in the cage is wild or nervous.

The above manner of maintaining heat is used by most fanciers, although they don't use the dimmer, just the bulb alone. A much better method of controlling heat is to use a short heating cable with a thermostat, which you may set to automatically maintain the temperature. Cover the cable with an inch of sand. A sick bird will benefit more this way by being directly over the heat. If too ill, it may lay right on the warm sand. Long heating cables are used in greenhouses and coldframes. You would require a smaller one, for which consult your poultry-appliance dealer or hardware store.

Perches in the hospital cage should be low, only two inches from the bottom.

Whichever heating system you install, your hospital cage will require a one-inch-high sheet-metal tray which may be slid in and out

Diseases and Health Problems

for cleaning.

The main treatment your bird will need is, first, heat 85 to 90 F.; and quiet, rest, and clean quarters second. This is basic to treating any illness.

Broken Legs

A broken leg requires three or four weeks to heal. In a small bird the leg may be set with a large-enough quill split along one side. With a pair of tweezers, put a few shreds of cotton inside the quill as padding. A small piece of transparent tape will hold it firmly. If you are all thumbs, cut the quill in half and do the job the same way. After much experimentation, I've found out that transparent tape makes the best binder for bandages and splints. It is almost invisible to the bird, doesn't attract its attention, and is so thin, binding so closely, that a fussy bird cannot pick it off as it would adhesive tape, thread, or string. Be careful not to get the transparent tape wet, however. When you wish to remove it, dip a piece of cotton in alcohol, applying it as you unwind it.

It is rare that the larger parrots or cockatoos break a leg. If one does, a splint must be made to fit around the leg without cutting off circulation. If you are inexperienced, it is much more advisable to bring your valuable parrot to a veterinarian who will do a skilled setting of the leg or wing. Treating a large psittacine will be a three-man job to hold it, unless it is skillfully anesthetized. When the leg is set in a splint, remove all perches for three weeks.

Broken Wings

A broken wing sometimes heals itself properly without treatment, if it just droops normally. If it hangs at an awkward angle, fold it against the bird's side and hold it in place by placing a strip of transparent tape twice around the body, leaving the other wing free. The tape may be removed easily with a piece of cotton dipped in alcohol.

Lice and Mites

If you followed the advice given in the first part of this book by giving your bird a monthly once-over, and dusting insecticide powder close to the body, it will never have lice. Don't leave a residue on top of the feathers. Perch ends, cage, and

Diseases and Health Problems

aviary corners should be cleaned every week or two with hot water and a disinfectant, or else touch these up with a brush dipped in kerosene or creosote, removing the birds till dry.

For scaly-leg mites, which are noticeable when your bird's legs and feet have rough-looking growth scales on them, apply either olive oil or mineral oil on the affected parts for three days. The old scales will loosen off, and the mites will be killed by the oil. Psittacine birds are rarely affected with scaly-leg mite as they clamber about a good deal. Passerine birds such as canaries, thrushes, etc., have legs more susceptible to attack by this mite.

Psittacosis or Ornithosis

A tiny virus-like microorganism causes this disease which was first discovered among newly imported parrots. When it occurs in birds outside of the parrot family, as in chickens or pigeons, it is known as ornithosis.

The signs in birds may include fever, thirst, fast breathing, and brownish droppings, which may turn green or bloody just before death. The bird eventually becomes emaciated and weak. This disease

requires diagnosis and treatment by a veterinarian, because the drugs now available to treat it require a prescription.

French Molt

This disease, first discovered in the mid 1880s, seems to be confined to Budgerigars, and almost entirely to young birds. It causes them to drop their flight and tail feathers either before or immediately after leaving the nest. Some birds eventually grow them again, but most never do. The body feathering also is usually defective with continual molting, and the birds are undersized. These afflicted birds are also called runners; being unable to fly, they always run along the bottom of the cage and clamber along the wire.

This disease has been said to be hereditary, although diet deficiencies seem to predispose towards it also. Some authorities now believe it is caused by a microorganism. Affected birds should not be used for breeding, and when purchasing Budgies, inquire into the past history of the birds regarding french molt. Often some of the young will be afflicted while another brood will be normal. Much remains to be

Diseases and Health Problems

known about this disease, and no sure cure is known. Feed your birds a complete diet as recommended with a daily pinch of vitamin-mineral powder, especially 2 to 3 months before and during the breeding season. The poor-diet possibility will at least be eliminated.

Enteritis

This is a highly contagious intestinal disease often caused by overcrowding and filthy, unsanitary quarters, perches, and water receptacles. This applies to newly imported birds in a shipment as well as to a fancier's collection. This condition may be suspected when birds are inactive and quiet, with ruffled-up feathers. The bird eats but is emaciated, and feels light when picked up.

When thus discovered, the bird should be immediately placed in a hospital cage with 85 to 90 F. temperature day and night. The cage or aviary should be sprayed or washed down with a strong solution of disinfectant. Feed and water receptacles should be washed daily in hot water and washing soda. A pinch of either epsom salts or sodium perborate may be given in the drinking water for 2 to 3 days.

If you have a large breeding collection, your veterinarian may provide you with whichever drugs will best treat the illness. When cleaning your pens, replace the birds only when everything is thoroughly dry. This disease is another reason why you should quarantine newly purchased birds 3 to 4 weeks before placing them in your collection.

Colds

Your bird has a cold because it is placed in a draft. A cheerful sunny window is a good spot only if there isn't too much breeze, particularly on a cold day when the window should be closed.

Sick birds have ruffled plumage, with the head often "under the wing." It may be heard to sneeze and sniffle when breathing. A tiny blob of medicated petroleum jelly may be placed in the beak with a toothpick. With this same toothpick, apply a small amount of nose drops on each nostril. Place the bird immediately in your hospital cage at 85 to 90 F. for a week or two till cured. If you don't have such a cage, keep the bird near or, if it isn't too hot, over the radiator. Another treatment is to cover the cage and allow the fumes from a hot teakettle's spout to enter from the bottom of the cage. A menthol ointment may be placed in the kettle with a little water.

Pneumonia

An untreated cold may lead to pneumonia, the signs of which are the same as for a cold, except that the lungs are affected, and the bird gasps for breath. Treatment by a veterinarian is the best hope. Carry the bird to him in your hospital cage, as it is imperative that it be kept at 85 to 90 F.

Feather Plucking and Care of Plumage

Some parrots are addicted to this bad habit. Some authorities claim that it is the lack of protein in the diet which causes the bird to crave for the taste of blood from its pin feathers, and suggest adding more protein to a parrot's diet to satisfy this need. A change of scenery is recommended, with a chance to fly if possible. Give the bird something to occupy itself with, such as a piece of a branch or block of wood.

It is best not to pull out a broken pinfeather, as a new one will be eventually sent out. If the feather is fully grown but defective, only then pull it out. Broken or worn flight and tail feathers may be pulled out, and will be replaced within a month. Only 2 or 3 feathers may be pulled out at one time. Pulling out too many may start feather plucking. When pulling out a wing feather, hold the wing firmly with the right hand at the base of the feather you are extracting, and pull the one feather out with a quick outward motion, so as not to hurt the wing.

Any bird may be started into preening its feathers by spraying with water from a mister. Some fanciers, when exhibiting at a bird show, put a few drops of glycerine in the water when spraying to give their birds a little sheen to the feathers. This isn't really necessary if your birds are on a good diet and in top condition.

Egg Binding

This trouble usually occurs in birds which are permitted to breed in cold weather. Lovebirds, and Budgies in particular, should have all nest boxes removed at the end of the breeding season or after the second or third brood is raised.

Diseases and Health Problems

Many commercial breeders separate the sexes, putting them in different flights at that time.

Egg binding can be brought on by sudden changes in the weather when the hen is ready to lay, causing spasmodic contractions of the uterus which in turn makes passage of the egg difficult. This may occur in warm weather also, if a hen is laying her first egg. A main cause is starting the breeding season too early. At the New York latitude, it is better to start breeding operations in the middle of March at the earliest.

The signs of egg binding are apparent when a hen is groggy in her actions, and stays on the cage floor straining to lay the egg. The egg may be felt as the lump in the abdomen.

The best method for removal is to place a drop or two of olive oil in the vent, then hold the bird over steam arising from a pan or teakettle spout of hot water for a few minutes without scalding the bird; after this, place the bird in its nest or in a heated hospital cage. If the egg is not passed, try the treatment again.

If you have skillful fingers and the egg still has not been ejected, it may be eased out by gentle pressure behind the egg. A few more drops of olive oil in the vent will help.

Claws and Bill

A nail clipper is the best instrument to use for trimming the tip of the upper mandible when it grows too long. Clip along the sides of the upper mandible near the tip, leaving a point. If your psittacine bird has been given a block of wood or piece of branch to exercise its bill on, this will be less of a problem.

Claws are trimmed with clippers by first holding each claw up to the light so you may see where the claw is solid and where the vein is. Trim off at an angle at this point.

As the author of this book, I hope to see more of the U.S. public take up the absorbing hobby of bird keeping and breeding, whether for pleasure or profit.

Under the strains of daily life, we all need to escape into a little world of our own making, where tension and strife are forgotten during the time we spend with an engrossing hobby.

Bird keeping and breeding supplies this need for relaxation from daily irritations, and adds interest to the art of living and enjoying life.